RUDE
AWAKENING

TONI McCLOE

RUDE
AWAKENING

TATE PUBLISHING
AND ENTERPRISES, LLC

Published by Tate Publishing & Enterprises, LLC
127 E. Trade Center Terrace | Mustang, Oklahoma 73064 USA
1.888.361.9473 | www.tatepublishing.com

Tate Publishing is committed to excellence in the publishing industry. The company reflects the philosophy established by the founders, based on Psalm 68:11,
"The Lord gave the word and great was the company of those who published it."

Published in the United States of America

ISBN: 978-1-63268-136-2
Family & Relationships / Love & Romance
14.05.16

For my children: Eric, Cynthia, and Jessica
And for Don

ACKNOWLEDGMENTS

For everyone who helped and supported me while I wrote this book, I want to say thank you.

To Tate Publishing for taking my dream of writing a book from the ethereal into the physical.

To my children for giving me a computer, to Cynthia and Jessica for being my first editors and most ardent supporters, and to Eric for believing in me and encouraging me to write.

To Morton Axelrod, thanks for giving me a push in the right direction and for teaching me everything I needed to know.

To Barbara Weber for teaching me how to define myself and then how to expand that definition.

To my sisters for sharing with me their memories and insights.

To my writing teachers: Richard D. Bank, for making me work harder, and Kristina Moriconi, for reminding me that words *are* music.

To the members of my writing group: Kelly, Alejandra, Doreen, Pam, and Neal, who held my hands whenever they were not typing or poised above the keyboard.

AUTHOR'S NOTE

This story is a depiction of my life as I remember it. Some names and details have been changed to protect the privacy of others.

CONTENTS

PART 1: GROWING UP CRAZY

The Child Who Disappeared.. 17
Word Salad.. 22
Bloody Bones... 27
Dark Streaks on a Tombstone.. 37
A Child Forgotten... 45
The Pane Between Us 51
Boys Have Short Hair, Girls Wear Dresses 55
Blinking Lights and Shooting Stars....................................... 61
The Ten-Dollar Loaf of Italian Bread.................................... 69
From Jekyll to Hyde 76

PART 2: THERAPY

Ten Perfect Fingers and Ten Perfect Toes 89
Why My Mother Was Angry 95
Dr. Phil and Chopra 102
The Madness of the Gods.. 113
Like What Rumi Said About Lovers.................................... 116
In Paper Cups Instead of China 122
What I Always Wanted 126

PART 3: RUDE AWAKENING

In Solitude and In Silence 137
The Rosetta Stone.. 147
What Was in the Chasm 152
In a Dance Together 155

EPILOGUE

His Name Was Don 161

From left to right: Uncle Nicky, Aunt Nancy, my grandfather John, my mother Lily, Aunt Clara, and my grandmother Angelina. The picture was taken before Aunt Margaret was born, probably in late 1917 or early 1918.

GROWING UP CRAZY

I will speak to you from my memory—my memory—a memory that is all refracting light slanting through prisms and dreams, a shifting, troubled riot of electrons charged with pain and wonder.

—Pat Conroy

THE CHILD WHO DISAPPEARED

My mother kept secrets. "Don't ever let your left hand know what your right hand is doing," she would tell me when I was little. I would watch her then as she plunged her hands into warm, soapy water or use them to stretch pizza or pasta dough for dinner, all the while wondering how one of her hands could not possibly know what the other was doing.

But my mother knew. Her deepest secret—the one concerning my grandmother's death—was the one she kept for more than seventy years. Once revealed, it became the Rosetta Stone for understanding my own life.

Had I known when I got off the elevator that day back in 2003 that I had just taken the first step toward uncovering that secret, I may not have been so reluctant. As it was, I got off the elevator and walked down the corridor slowly, examining every door until I found the one I wanted. Inside, a card on an empty desk told me to have a seat. My doctor—it said—would be with me shortly.

I sat on a straight-backed chair and reached for a magazine. I paged through it listlessly, then tossed it aside. I stared at a Monet on the wall opposite me as classical music streamed from a boom box, sitting on an end table, but nothing held my interest or calmed me as I sat on the edge of the chair, wondering what I was doing there.

The clock on the wall said 9:57. My appointment was scheduled for ten. I had three minutes in which to decide if I wanted to stay or if I wanted to bolt. After all, I had tried this solution before and had received nothing more than a temporary Band-Aid for my injuries. This time, I wanted more.

I jumped up, walked to a window, and stood there, watching as torrential amounts of rain fell onto the intersection below. The rain comforted me as it always had. I stood there for a while longer, thinking about a time when I was small and still believed in "happily ever after."

Behind me, I heard footsteps. I turned to see a man in a light gray suit and a white shirt, opened at the collar. He extended his hand, introducing himself, then turned and led me down another corridor to his office where he raised his hand again to indicate the seats inside the room.

"Please," he said, "make yourself comfortable."

I stepped inside and studied my surroundings. The most prominent feature there was a built-in bookcase that ran the entire length of one wall. The sight of so many books comforted me. There were classics as well as books on philosophy and psychology. There were also books on spirituality, some of which I had already read. A cluster of books at the extreme right concerned death and dying, and I gravitated toward it.

"I have a friend," I said, still standing in front of the books. Then I stopped and turned around. "Does everyone always start that way?" I asked the therapist who was still standing in the doorway.

He smiled as I took a seat on the sofa. He chose the recliner opposite me. "Please, tell me about your friend."

"I have a friend," I said, glancing again at the bookcase, "who says she's afraid of dying. But then, isn't everyone?" I asked, expecting him to answer, expecting him to have an exact count. When he didn't answer, I continued, "Except I'm not."

He smiled, a grown up indulging a child.

"Anyway, that's not why I'm here," I said, raising my hand and waving it dismissively. "That's not what I wanted to talk about."

He said nothing, waiting for me to continue.

"I'm here," I said, wondering if I looked as nervous as I felt, "because both my mother and my lover have been behaving in ways that make me feel abandoned. Actually, they make me feel invisible.

"My mother has Alzheimer's, and she doesn't recognize me. She's in a nursing home. The other day, while visiting her, I asked if she knew who I was. She looked at me and said no. A moment later, when my sister walked through the door, my mother smiled at her and spoke her name." I fell silent for a moment before I continued. "I grew up in the fifties, and my parents were strict. I had four sisters, and we may as well have grown up in a convent. Actually, I was in a convent but—" I stopped suddenly to look at this man. *Who is he?* I wondered, *and how do I relate to him?* He was tall and handsome, a well-built man with salt and pepper hair and movie star good looks and not much younger than I was.

"It was before Mary Tyler Moore threw her hat into the air. Besides, my parents were first generation Italian," I added as though that explained everything. He looked at me but said nothing. "You know. Old school," I said as clarification.

"A little while ago, you said you felt abandoned. Can you elaborate on that?" he asked. "Tell me more about how that makes you feel."

"Lonely," I answered. "It makes me feel lonely. Not long ago, I was living in the mother-in-law suite of my youngest daughter's house. My daughter lived upstairs with her husband and four children, while I lived downstairs with my mother.

"When my mother went to live with my sister, I decided I wanted to live independently and began looking for an apartment. I wanted something close to my daughter and grandchildren, but something I could afford." I hesitated, then looked directly at the therapist and asked, "Can I tell you about a dream I had?"

"Of course."

"It isn't too Freudian to tell you my dreams?"

He laughed, and I continued. "One night, while I was looking, I dreamt I found an apartment I liked that was nearby and within my budget. In the dream, the apartment was on the second floor, and while standing in the living room, I could hear people talking. I walked to the window and looked down.

"There was a lake below with people who were enjoying the sunshine. Just below the window, two men were teaching a beautiful, blond-headed little boy to swim. The boy looked to be about three, maybe four years old, and as he became more adept in the water, the men paid less and less attention to him.

"The second floor window gave me an advantage the men didn't have, and I could see he was getting tired. Suddenly, he disappeared beneath the water's surface. I started pounding on the window, but no one heard me. I opened my mouth to scream, but no sound emerged.

"The lake began filling with people, looking for the little boy. Suddenly everything went silent—you know how things can change in a dream without warning."

He nodded as I continued, "It appeared to be later. The sun was going down, and it was almost dark. All activity stopped and a deep, deafening silence filled the air. I realized all hope was gone, and I began to cry. When I woke up, there were tears running down my face and onto the pillow. I wanted to go back to sleep to find a new ending for my dream, but I couldn't. My alarm was about to go off, and I had to get ready for work."

"What do you think the dream meant?"

"At the time, I wasn't sure. Then, six months ago, I found an apartment just like the one in my dream, and like the one in my dream, it was on the second floor. It was located on several acres of land that had once been a farm, and at the time, I loved its isolation. It was just a short drive from my daughter's house, and best of all, it was fifty dollars a month less than in my dream. The day I moved in, I walked to the living room window and noticed a swimming pool in the yard below. And that's when I knew."

"Knew what?"

"That the beautiful little boy in my dream represented love— the love I was losing."

"Whose love?" he asked. But I wasn't ready yet to talk about Vincent.

WORD SALAD

It was my second meeting with the therapist I had begun thinking of as Dr. A. Although I was still nervous, I was looking forward to another session with him. Thinking about the first reminded me how good it felt to talk about my feelings, to be encouraged to talk about my feelings.

The doctor greeted me when I arrived, then sent me on ahead, saying he would join me in a couple of minutes. I entered the room amazed again at the number of books inside. I was just removing one from its shelf when the doctor came into the room.

"Have you read all of these books?" I asked.

He shook his head. "Not yet," he said, "not all of them."

"Have you read this one?" I asked, holding the book so he could read its title. It was Nicholas Delbanco's *Old Scores*.

He smiled.

"It's one of my favorites," I said, opening the book to the beginning as I walked to the sofa. "Even the first two lines are as haunting as the rest of the story." We talked about the book for a few minutes until I felt relaxed enough to continue. "Where were we last week?" I asked.

He shook his head. "We don't have to do it that way," he said as he took his seat across from me. "You can talk about anything. Start anywhere." But I was intent on remembering where we had ended the week before.

"How was your week?" he asked, interrupting my thoughts.

I sighed. "I went to see my mother," I said, placing my hands on my knees as though to brace myself. "But it was difficult. I hate seeing her there. I hate seeing her that way." I had been looking down, but now I looked up as though expecting his words to fix everything.

"What way?"

"Empty. Vacant." A shiver went through me. We were both silent a moment before he spoke again.

"When you were here last week, you mentioned someone else," he said. I looked at him not sure who he meant. "You spoke about a lover. What can you tell me about him?" I sighed, still not ready to talk about Vincent. Instead, I looked at the book I was holding, studying its contents until I realized I was looking for some way to change the subject.

"I had another lover once," I said, still looking at the book. "It was a long time ago, and he had just come back from Vietnam." I closed the Delbanco book and got up to return it to its place on the shelf. I reached out to touch another book, but changed my mind and returned to my seat across from the doctor.

"In Vietnam, there had been an explosion of some kind, and he was locked inside a cave with two other men, both of whom were members of the Vietcong." I had been looking down as I spoke, but now I looked up again at the doctor, who was leaning forward in his chair, listening intently. "After the explosion, he remembered nothing until he woke up in a psychiatric hospital where he was diagnosed paranoid schizophrenic." I glanced at Dr. A, expecting him to speak, but he said nothing.

"I had known this man before he went to Vietnam, but when he returned, things were different. He was different. Sometimes, we would sit on the sofa, talking, and the room would get dark, but neither of us would turn on the lamp. Then suddenly, he would—I'm not sure how to describe it—he would be talking, but his words"—I hesitated—"they weren't making sense. No." I said, correcting myself. "The words made sense. They were *actual* words, but they didn't fit together. They didn't form sentences."

"Word salad," Dr. A interjected.

"What?"

"Word salad," he repeated. "That's what psychiatrists call it. But please go on."

I nodded. "Sometimes, we would sit and talk this way for a few minutes until I reached over to turn on the lamp, which seemed to bring him back to himself, and he would laugh. It was a short laugh filled with irony and"—I hesitated again—"contempt, I think, and he would say something, like 'I bet you don't know what I'm talking about,' as though he'd been explaining something too difficult for me to understand."

"When this happened, what were you thinking?" Dr. A asked, still sitting forward in his chair.

"I was afraid. I knew instinctively that he had gone back inside that cave. I knew that's where his mind was, and I was afraid."

"What were you afraid of?"

"Of the madness," I said, looking directly at the doctor. "I was afraid of the madness inside him and inside myself."

"Of the madness," Dr. A said, echoing my words and speaking softly, as though to himself. He sat back, then drummed his fingers absently on the arm of the recliner. "Do you think the madness could be something else?" he asked. I looked at him, unsure of his meaning.

"Like loneliness?" he suggested.

I looked down at my hands and said nothing. Then I glanced up at the doctor, who was sitting quietly waiting for an answer. "Tell me about the loneliness."

"Sometimes," I said, speaking slowly. "I think the loneliness is a punishment for something—for some inconsiderate act I performed in the past or for some act I failed to perform.

"Sometimes, I think I'm alone because of some deal I made with the devil or with God, and I wonder if I wanted something so much a long time ago that I was willing to bargain away companionship in order to gain whatever trinket it was I wanted then?" I hesitated and looked at the doctor. He nodded, encouraging me to go on.

"I know that life is supposed to take you down a path, a path that only God wants you on, and I think, *Is this where you want me, God? Here? Really? You seem so sure, God, while I am sure of nothing—least of all my own sanity.*

"There are times," I said, closing my eyes, "when I wake up in the middle of the night, not knowing where I am or even who I am until I hear the sound of my own breathing. Then, like a magician, I begin to conjure a world all around me, a world separate from the instant in which there was nothing, and I find myself wondering which one is real."

I opened my eyes and looked at the bookcase to my left and then at the therapist. "But there is one thing I do know. I know I won't find the answers I'm looking for in a book or outside that window. I need to find them here," I said, raising my hand to indicate the space between us. "And I need your help."

We continued talking then, the doctor and me. It was a conversation that was to continue over the next five years. When I was a child, my favorite toy was a kaleidoscope. I used to love looking into it, turning the bottom of it and watching as the tiny pieces of glass changed from one mirrored image into another.

Therapy with Dr. A was like that for me. Each time I went, I watched as the image I held of myself changed until finally, I could see myself, not as the split and fractured personality I was when it began, but as the whole and healthy human being I was becoming when it ended.

"What was your childhood like?" Dr. A asked at the beginning of our next session.

I closed my eyes for a moment, then opened them again. "When I was four years old, I went to a birthday party held for one of my cousins. In those days, little girls got all dressed up for parties. So I was dressed in a white taffeta dress with stiff, starched crinolines underneath to make it stand out as far as possible. The dress had large purple polka dots all over it." I smiled and looked at Dr. A, who smiled too.

"At the party, there was a poster in the room with a picture of a donkey on it." I looked beyond Dr. A and stared at the wall behind him.

"Who wants to be first?" my aunt asked. Hearing only the word "first" and not really knowing what I was volunteering for, I shot my arm up immediately.

"Good," she said. Then she took me by the hand and led me to the center of the room where she covered my eyes with a blindfold. All the other girls in the room giggled and laughed as she handed me a paper tail and spun me around in circles. "Okay," she said. "Go pin the tail on the donkey."

I took my eyes from the wall and focused on Dr. A. "I started moving forward, but when I heard the girls' laughter getting louder, I decided I was headed in the wrong direction. I tried again with my hands out in front of me, trying to feel something solid, but I just kept coming up with empty space.

"I was dizzy after being spun around in circles. With the blindfold on, I felt a scary feeling. I felt the way Alice must have felt just after she stepped through the looking glass. I had no idea where I was or in which direction I should go. Which is pretty much how I felt for most of my childhood."

BLOODY BONES

It's amazing how much I remember about the first neighborhood I lived in, especially if you consider I lived in it for only eight years, seven if you don't count the year I spent in the hospital. We were living in North Philadelphia then, where Reese Street meets Glenwood Avenue. My father owned the beer distributor on that corner. The entrance to the store was on Glenwood, and the door leading to the apartment above the store was around the corner on Reese Street. I seem to remember lying in my crib, listening for the sound of my father's voice as he came up the stairs from work. As soon as I heard it, I would pull myself up, jump up and down, and shake the railings of my crib until he came into the room to rescue me. He always came into the room to rescue me. Then, off we would go on some exciting adventure together, even if it were only into the dining room for dinner.

I have another, more vivid memory of seeing a small plane smashing itself into the house across the street and of seeing the house and the plane burst into flames. I can remember the screams of the fire engines and the sizzling sound the water made as it streamed from the hoses and struck the flames. I remember the heat of the fire and the height of the flames, and even though I was only two years old, I remember all of this happening because it was the only time I can remember being held in my mother's arms.

I remember too, a Friday afternoon in 1945, just before the war ended. I was almost four then and not yet able to read, but I knew the words that said "Ortliebs" and "Schmidts" and other words printed on the heavy cardboard boxes that were delivered to the store almost daily. I knew too that the red neon sign in the window said "open" when it was on and nothing when it went out.

It was a warm day, early in April, and I was sitting on the front stoop, waiting for my sisters, Gina and Marie, to come home from school. I was safe there on Reese Street, a tiny little street too narrow for automobiles. The only traffic there came during the early morning hours when our street was busy with peddlers, pulling their carts or with men seated behind horse-drawn wagons.

Outside I could hear the voices of the farmers as they called out the names of the things they grew, making words such as watermelon and strawberries; and even corn on the cob sounds like music.

I watched as the milkman inched forward with his black shiny horse that always looked straight ahead, even when I stood beside him or when I reached out to touch him, tentatively. There were times when the humidity made the street so steamy, the piles of waste left by the horses became malodorous. The buzzing of the flies, hovering above them seemed to grow louder as the day's heat intensified.

I could hear too the whirl of the grinder when the knifeman came to sharpen our knives, and I saw the cart the ragman pulled. If I were inside when the ragman called, my mother would tell me to grab the old clothes sitting by the door. Then I would run outside to meet him and watch as he piled them on top of the others. When he pulled away, I could see the sleeves of our garments hanging over the sides, sliding along the ground behind him.

Later, after the peddlers were gone and the street was clean, my sisters would return with the other neighborhood children and Reese Street would become the playground on which we played with our bats and balls or with our chalk and jump ropes.

That day started out no different from any other day. While I waited for my sisters, I watched as some of the men and older boys from the neighborhood (Gina always called them the "four-effers") played a game in which they took turns tossing a pair of dice against a brick wall that stood at the end of the block. I must have gotten too close to their game that afternoon because as I watched, they froze the way my sisters and I did when we played statues.

"Don't pay any attention to her," one of the older men said. "She's too young to remember what she's seeing. Besides, she's Nick's girl, and she won't rat on us." A man dressed in a ragged shirt and overalls rolled above his ankles picked up the dice and threw them hard against the wall. "Sonna ma beach," he said when they landed. Another man with patches on the knees of his pants and stubble on his chin picked up the dice and blew on them, yelling "Snake eyes," as he slammed them against the wall.

There was always one man among the group who stood with his back to the others, "playing lookout." Whenever one of the city's bright red police cars passed slowly by the top of the street, the lookout would start whistling and rocking back and forth on his heels. Then all the other men and boys would turn around quickly with their hands behind their backs, and they would start rocking and whistling too.

I got bored watching them and started counting the squares in the sidewalk as I walked back to the other end of the street. When I arrived, I saw my sisters returning from school. Marie, who was nineteen months older than I was, was at least a half a block ahead of Gina. Marie was all lines and angles, elbows and knees, while Gina, who was a year older than Marie, was plump and round and as soft as a pillow. Both girls wore their hair in pigtails and both were dressed in white blouses and dark blue uniforms imprinted with the name of their school, St. Veronica's.

"What were you doing?" Marie asked when she saw me.

"I was counting the squares," I told her. "Like Gina taught me," I added. Gina had told me that one to twenty were numbers. She said the world was full of numbers, and if you could string them all together like lights on a Christmas tree, they would reach from here to heaven. "I was walking to heaven," I said.

"You can't walk all the way to heaven," Gina, who had just caught up with us, said.

"Besides," Marie added, "you have to get dead before you can get to heaven."

"No, you don't," I said, not quite sure what dead meant.

"Yes, you do," she insisted. But I knew she was wrong because our dad told me Marie didn't see the world the way I did. Marie sucked her thumb and when she did, her index and middle fingers formed a *V* in front of her eyes, and my dad said she could see only the world between those two fingers.

Gina sucked her thumb too, but only at night and only sometimes. Marie had a speech defect that made her shy, and like our mom, she almost never smiled. But Gina had a smile that lit up her face the way the word "open" lit up the store window.

The next morning was Saturday, the day on which my sisters and I walked to the Free Library of Philadelphia that had two white, stone lions, guarding its entrance on Lehigh Avenue. Once there, Gina and I picked out books she would read to me at bedtime. After that, we walked to the Century Theater to watch a double feature. Sometimes, when there was just one movie, we would watch it twice or until it was time to go home for dinner.

As we arrived at the intersection where the movie theater was, I could see the entire marquee from across the street. In front of the theater, I looked at the posters. "I'm not going in there," I announced.

"Why not?" Gina asked.

"She's afraid of the dark!" Marie said after taking her thumb from her mouth.

"No, I'm not," I retorted.

"Then why won't you go inside?" Gina asked.

"Because," was the only answer I could muster. I was not going to tell them I was not afraid of the dark. I knew they wouldn't believe me, but I wasn't. Well, I wasn't as afraid of the dark as I was of the quicksand. From the pictures outside the theater, I knew there was going to be quicksand, but the men on the screen never knew it was there until it was too late. Then I would have to watch as they fell into it.

Gina and Marie grabbed me by the arms and dragged me inside where I had to watch—between my fingers—as the men began sinking. I started screaming then until Gina put her hand over my mouth and told me to stop.

"Close your eyes," she said, "and count to five." I did as I was told, but even with my eyes closed, I knew there would be nothing left of those men to see except their arms stretched high above their heads. By the time we left the theater, I just knew that when we got home that night I'd be scared the way I was most Saturday nights. I'd get so scared I'd start screaming until Gina shook me awake and told me I was dreaming.

When we returned from the movie theater, my sisters and I hung our jackets on hooks under the hallway mirror and headed for the kitchen, knowing our mother would be there. She was always in the kitchen preparing a meal or washing dishes. But she seemed not to mind doing all the cooking and cleaning.

She was in her early thirties then with a body that was plump, but not in the same way Gina's was. My mother's roundness was confined to her stomach, which protruded under the apron she wore to protect her dress. Gina said she would lose that plumpness after she got back from the hospital where she would have to go to get our new baby brother or sister.

When we got to the kitchen, we saw her standing in front of the sink with her back to us. She had rolled her stockings down to her ankles, making it easy for me to see the purple veins that crisscrossed along the backs of her legs. She turned after hearing us come in but said nothing. She was too busy, I think, stirring a pot on the stove. Finally, she told us to wash up. Afterward, we returned to the table in silence. Our mother liked silence, especially at the table where she was always telling us that children should be seen and not heard. The problem with that, however, was that most of the time, she didn't seem to be seeing or hearing my sisters and me.

My mom served us pasta three times a week—every Sunday, Tuesday, and Thursday. Because it was Saturday night, my sisters and I were expecting lentils and rice or pigs in the blanket for dinner, but Mom surprised us with canned soup, toasted cheese sandwiches, and left over icebox cake for dessert.

"Eat," she said, "then get into your pajamas and ready for bed." She said it was her turn to go out. She and our father were going out with Uncle Nicky and his wife. "Your cousin, Joanie, is coming to babysit."

Uncle Nicky was my mother's brother and her oldest sibling. Last Christmas after my dad brought home the new dining room table with the three extensions he made for the holidays, my mom cooked the Feast of the Seven Fishes. By six o'clock, all the extensions were in the new table and all the chairs were filled, except two. Uncle Nicky had not yet arrived, and my father had just gone downstairs to make sure the door to the store was locked.

When Uncle Nicky finally walked through the door, everyone turned to look at him. He looked funny, walking toward the table. He looked as though he did not know which way to go. His left leg seemed to be moving right; his right, left.

"It's about time," my mother said, giving him the look she gave to me whenever she thought I was about to do something I was not supposed to do. Uncle Nicky ignored her. He pulled an empty chair away from the table. As he sat down, the chair croaked and groaned under his weight, and he ended up on the floor.

The grown-ups started yelling all at once in English and in Italian, while my cousins imitated his walk and his fall. On the floor, my uncle looked broken, like a puppet whose strings had been cut. He looked as though he did not understand what had happened. Actually, he looked the way I had after I'd been blindfolded at my cousin's birthday party.

Finally, my father came into the room, and after seeing my uncle on the floor, helped him into another chair he brought in from the kitchen. My mother said something in Italian I did not understand. She often spoke in Italian, even to me, although I did not understand the words. Sometimes her words, even the ones spoken in English, made me feel far removed from her as though I existed at the other end of a long tunnel that kept me far away from her. After she spoke to my uncle in Italian, she said something in English I did not understand either. She said something about an apple that had fallen not far away from a tree.

All the noise and confusion frightened me that day. As a four-year-old, I didn't understand why everyone was laughing and shouting, nor did I understand what was wrong with my uncle. It was not until I was a teenager watching James Dean stagger to the banquet table in the last scenes of his movie career that I remembered that day and understood that my uncle was as drunk as Jett in *Giant*.

When my uncle arrived to go to the movies that night, he was with his wife Mary and his daughter Joanie. I watched to see if he were about to fall again, but he did not look as though he would. He was standing straight and tall as he waited for my parents. Just before the grown-ups left, my mom told Joanie to get us to bed early so we would be sure to wake up for church in the morning, and Joanie said, "Fine, no problem."

There was a piano just inside our apartment, separating the living room from the dining room. I am not sure why we had a piano since no one knew how to play it, but because our last name was Caruso, I think my dad hoped one of us would one day show some musical ability. The only person to ever use that piano was Joanie who, as soon as our parents left, walked to the front door of the apartment, opened it, and counted the steps to the landing below. There were thirteen steps.

Leaving the door open, Joanie walked back to the piano, lifted the cover from the keys, struck the deepest, darkest one and announced, "Bloody Bones is coming to get you." Then she hit another key and said, "Bloody Bones is on the first step." Another and Bloody Bones was on the second step. Before Bloody Bones reached the sixth step, we were all in our room and under the covers. Between Bloody Bones and the quicksand, I knew that I was going to have my choice of nightmares and that I was going to wake up screaming before the night was over.

That night, I was tired from all the walking we had done, and I fell asleep easily, at least until the middle of the night when I heard screams I was pretty sure were not coming from me. I sat up in the bed I shared with my sisters and looked through the curtained window as a bolt of lightning lit up the midnight sky. I listened to the thunder, rumbling in the distance until I heard the screams again. This time, I knew they were coming from the parlor.

My eyes grew wide apart as I listened with all my might to a strange voice that sounded like the hissing noise our teakettle made when the water got too hot. Too frightened to listen any longer, I wrapped the covers around my head and hid under the pillow. But I could still hear that voice.

I couldn't move. My lungs felt empty. My stomach moved up and down faster and faster until suddenly I knew that voice. It was Mommy's voice. I removed the covers from my head and listened to my mother's angry voice.

"I don't want her here," my mother screamed. "She doesn't belong here. Take her away."

Who was Mommy talking about? I wondered. *Was she talking about me?*

"Gina," I whispered, placing my hand on my sister's back. But I got no response. I slipped from beneath the covers and moved to the bottom of the bed. I was afraid, but less afraid now that I was moving. Through the partially opened door, I could see my father sitting on the couch. My mother was standing above him with one finger pointed in his direction.

I could hear my father's voice, but not his words. *Where are his words?* I wondered. His voice sounded little, like the lady's voice—the lady who stood barefoot on the corner, speaking to strangers and asking for money. Whenever my mother saw her, she called her a gypsy.

My heart was pounding so loud I was sure my mother would hear it. I turned and raced back to the bed. "Ouch," Gina said as I tried to jump over her aiming for the space I had vacated earlier.

"Gina, what's happening?" I asked.

"Mommy and Daddy are fighting?" she said as she started to straighten the covers I'd messed up when I got out of bed.

"About me?"

"No, silly. About Delores. Mommy doesn't want her here."

"But Gina, Delores is our sister."

"She's our half sister, and Mommy doesn't like her."

"Mommy doesn't like me too."

"Yes, she does. Besides, Daddy likes you. I heard Mommy telling Aunt Clara you're his favorite."

"But Gina, isn't Delores Daddy's favorite?"

"That's different."

"Why?"

"I don't know," Gina admitted. "Just go back to sleep," she said as she put her thumb back into her mouth, ending the conversation. I turned to my right where Marie was lying. She hadn't moved. She seemed to be sleeping with her thumb in her mouth.

I put my head back down on the pillow, convinced my mother was talking about me. I balled my hands into fists and held them against my cheeks, determined not to cry. From the parlor, I heard my daddy crying. I heard my daddy crying, and I was crying too. *Don't worry, Daddy,* I thought, *when I grow up, Delores can come and live with me.*

I glanced at the clock behind Dr. A's head. "It's almost time to quit," I said as I reached for my coat. It was mid-January, and by now, I had been in therapy for several months.

He smiled. "In a moment," he said. "First, tell me what made you think your mother was talking about you?"

"When I looked into the parlor," I said, "I didn't see Delores, so I thought she was talking about me. I started wondering then if mothers could do that. If they could send little children away. I thought my mother had sent Delores away because she didn't live with us, and I wondered if that was going to happen to me."

It was cold outside, and I had already put my arms through the sleeves of my coat. I was pulling on my gloves when Dr. A put his hands on the arms of his chair and got ready to rise.

"But it didn't happen to you," he said.

"No, Dr. A," I said, "you're wrong. It did happen to me."

DARK STREAKS ON A TOMBSTONE

The war in Europe ended a couple of weeks later. When our neighbors heard the news on their radios, they all ran outside to celebrate. Gina, Marie, and I watched from the window upstairs as they started dancing in the streets. Gina said people had been looking for something to celebrate for a long time. She said it had not helped much when the president died in April except in our house because our new baby sister was born a day earlier at the hospital where our mom had gone to find her.

That night, when the war ended, our dad was still at work, and our mother was in the bedroom with baby Joanne. As my sisters and I watched from the window, someone grabbed a rope and put it around his neck—the monster's neck. The monster in the brown suit with the tiny moustache on his face and eyes that looked empty as they stared up at us from where he got hung on the lamppost.

"He's dead," I screamed, and Gina laughed.

"It's a dummy, dummy," she said. "They're pretending he's Hitler."

A man with an accordion was playing the "Beer Barrel Polka." When he stopped, people were screaming. I saw bottles sail through the air and heard the sound of glass breaking. Fists started flying in every direction.

"You sonna ma beach," Mr. Amici yelled when Mr. Krauss told him his people had green horns. Then, Mr. Martini went and stood under Hitler. Mr. Martini was the man all the kids called Mussolini when he came stumbling up the street at night. Whenever I saw him coming, I would hide behind my father.

"Don't call him names," my father told me. "He's just a young man who went off to war and came back an old man."

I watched as Mr. Martini stood under Hitler, grabbed his rope, made him shake, and made him dance. Then, Mr. Martini started to laugh and started to shake all over. He laughed so hard he had to sit on the curb and cover his eyes, which made his shoulders start shaking too. When Hitler looked down at the crowd, he was shaking all over. Hitler kept shaking and laughing until someone cut his rope and carried him away.

My sisters and I heard sirens and saw the red lights that swirled in circles on top of the paddy wagons as they stopped at the top of the street. The police jumped from their vehicles trying to end the free for all as the neighbors went running back to their houses. Someone ran up the stairs to our apartment, rang the doorbell, and ran back down again. When Mommy, who had not been paying much attention to the noise outside, opened the door, we heard her blood-curdling scream. We turned from the window just in time to see her fall backward as the Hitler dummy fell on top of her.

In addition to owning the beer distributor downstairs, my father worked as a carpenter and a cabinetmaker in South Philadelphia where he designed and made furniture and cabinets for use in museums and homes all around the country and, according to Gina, for "that thin man in Hollywood."

My dad was a small man, standing just over five feet with hair that was beginning to thin and turn gray at the temples. When he worked, he wore plaid flannel shirts in muted colors tucked into baggy pants that were held up with suspenders. When he spoke, it was with an accent for although he had been born in this country, his family had returned to Italy when he was just two years old.

The village they returned to was San Giacomo degli Schiavoni located in the province of Campobasso in the hills of Southern Italy. It was located three miles inland from the coastal town of Termoli. Growing up, my father could stand outside the front door of his home and look to the west to see the mountains running down the center of the country or to the east to see the calm coastline of the Adriatic Sea.

At the time of their emigration, in 1906, most of the land in Italy belonged to either the rich or the religious, neither of which included my grandparents. When they left Italy, they left to keep from starving. Upon their return, they discovered that conditions had not improved.

My grandmother died a year after their return, and when my grandfather remarried, seven more children were born into the family. All ten children and the two adults lived in a two-room flat with a loft where the children slept. Later, my father would tell me how, during World War I, he would listen to the sounds of the German bombers, flying overhead as they competed with the rumbling sounds inside his own empty belly.

"Nicholas! Nicholas!" his youngest sister called as she came running through the village one day in 1926. My father, who had just turned eighteen, was standing with a group of other young men, who were all staring into the distance, examining their futures. When his sister found him, she waved the letter she was holding in front of his face. "It's for you," she said in her lilting, little girl's voice.

"What is it?" he asked, annoyed and embarrassed that she had interrupted him while he was busy with his friends. After opening the envelope, he found it was a message from the Italian government informing him that he was about to be inducted into the army.

My father did not want to serve in Mussolini's army because he knew if he did, he would lose his American citizenship. After some deliberation with friends and family, he decided to leave Italy and return to the States where he would later meet my mother, Lillian Comparelli.

When I was growing up, the entire family ate dinner on Sundays at exactly one in the afternoon because my father wanted it that way. "That's the way it was done in the old country," he said.

During dinner, my father would sit at the table, telling my sisters and me stories about growing up in Italy. He delighted in telling us the story of Romulus and Remus, the twins who had been abandoned by their parents and who would later become the founders of the city of Rome. As my father talked, it was easy to tell he missed being back in Italy. He said he missed everything except the poverty.

When my father told us stories, he almost never included details about his life after he returned to America. I often sensed there was something about living here that my father was ashamed of. Sometimes when we talked, his shame felt so heavy, I felt as though I had to move away from him to keep it from falling onto me.

When my mother was growing up, her family attended a Presbyterian Church because it was the one closest to her house. When we were growing up, my mother sent my sisters and me to nine o'clock mass at St. Veronica's. Then at ten o'clock, she sent us to the Lutheran Church on the corner for Sunday school, and at eleven, we went to the Presbyterian Church for Bible study.

"Why do we have to go to three churches?" I asked my sisters one Sunday morning as we left the Lutheran Church and headed toward our Bible class. Marie just shrugged her shoulders and continued walking two steps ahead of me.

"Because Mommy needs time off," Gina said matter-of-factly.

Of the three churches, I preferred the quiet, hushed tones of the Catholic mass, but my sisters and cousins preferred the Lutheran Church where they loved to clap their hands and stomp their feet, bringing the walls of Jericho down with a crash or dramatically sending the Christian soldiers off to war. They laughed as they blew out the candles they were supposed to let shine in the darkness.

There were many Sundays, however, when, instead of going to church, we would pile into the back of my dad's DeSoto and head upstate to my grandmother's house in Pittston. My grandmother was never there, however, since she had died ten years before I was born.

Once off the main road, we took the dirt road that led directly to my grandmother's house. A cloud of dust arose and surrounded the car as it slowed and came to a stop. Once out of the car, chickens surrounded us because the chicken coop, which stood in the backyard, had a door with broken hinges, making it easy for those chickens to roam freely onto the road. The chickens were always the first ones to greet us. They ruled that backyard, and whenever my sisters and I played there, they would chase us and taunt us with their cackles.

Like my paternal grandparents, my mother's parents had also emigrated to Pittston in 1906, from another town in southern Italy called Vico del Gargano in the province of Foggia, just south of Campobasso. They fared well in Pittston where Giovanni, now known as John, worked as a coal miner and his wife, Angelina, opened a candy store in the basement of the house they bought together on Drummond Street. By the forties, however, both my grandmother and the candy store would be gone.

When we arrived at the house, we always entered it through the kitchen on the ground floor. The kitchen was the place where all the grown-ups gathered to talk animatedly in English and Italian, constantly interrupting one another as their hands clashed in midair. Whenever we arrived, my grandfather would always be sitting to the right of the door in a straight-backed chair that was flanked on one side by an ashtray and on the other by a spittoon. He was a tall, gaunt man who seemed bent and broken after too many years spent in the coalmines.

"You a gooda gal?" he would ask in his phlegm-filled voice that seemed deep and was gruffer than the stubble on his chin. Most of his teeth were missing. His question, which he asked using the only words he knew in English, never failed to intimidate me. I wanted nothing more than to escape as quickly as possible. My mother, however, would hold me by the shoulders until I acknowledged my grandfather and his toothless grin. My grandfather would reach for his papers and tobacco then, or he would start hacking uncontrollably, which was my cue to run from the room to the fresh air outside.

When dinner was ready, I had to return to the kitchen where either my mother or Aunt Mary, who had married my grandfather late in life after raising five boys of her own, would be standing by the coal stove, stroking the embers, clearing away ashes, and always cooking large quantities of food. Except for Aunt Mary, all the adults in the family spoke to one another in Italian. Not knowing the language, Aunt Mary seemed a misfit. But if she felt like one, she never showed it.

Aunt Mary wore her gray hair pulled back in a bun at the nape of her neck. She wore brightly colored, cotton dresses that came to the middle of her calves. When she spoke, the gold tooth in the upper corner of her mouth dazzled me. She was a happy-go-lucky kind of person who seemed oblivious to everything except her own place in the world. During dinner, which she served at a table that stood elevated on a platform to the left of the room, she kept up an easy banter, chuckling happily and often in a way that stood in sharp contrast to the rest of the adults in the family.

To the right of the stove was a door that opened into a dark, narrow room where the plumbing was first brought into the house. Before that, an outhouse was used. Its remains still stood in the backyard behind the chicken coop. That little room also held my grandmother's icebox with its huge block of ice taking up most of the space inside. Beyond that was the coal shoot with a pile of coal beneath it that varied in height from visit to visit and from season to season.

Just past my grandfather's chair was a partially hidden staircase, leading to the second floor where the empty parlor sat with its dusty over-stuffed, over-sized furniture that always made it seem as though the room needed a good airing. The second floor also held a single, darkened bedroom where my grandfather slept.

"This is the room where Grandmom died," Gina whispered into my ear one day. After that, whenever I passed that room, I would always close my eyes and walk on tiptoes, afraid even to peek inside, afraid that if I looked, I would see my grandmother, lying there as sick as she was the last time she slept there.

At the end of the hallway, a second staircase led to the top floor and a small bedroom where Uncle Nicky had slept as a child and to a larger room where my mother slept with her sisters. My sisters and I always stayed in the larger room whenever we stayed overnight in Pittston. But no matter how many times I slept in this room, it always felt strange to me. Inside this room, I felt a need to be held, a need more pronounced here than it would have been at home in my own room, surrounded by my own things. In this room, in this house, the darkness served only to accentuate the strangeness I felt inside myself and the strangeness of the objects that surrounded me, objects that had once belonged to my mother or to one of her sisters and had long ago been abandoned and forgotten.

Whenever we went upstate to Pittston, we visited my grandmother's grave located in the cemetery along the banks of the Susquehanna River where the coal was piled so high that for years, I believed those piles of coal were what the Pocono Mountains were made of. It was at the cemetery on Decoration Day at the end of May one year that my mother told me for the first time about my grandmother's death. She put her hand on my arm, and as she began talking about the day her mother died, her fingers tightened around my bicep.

"Before she died," my mother said, "she told us she wanted a band to play at her funeral. My father hired Cino Paci's band to lead the cortege from our home to the church and then to the cemetery." While my mother talked, everything around me grew deep and quiet. It wasn't until after she stopped talking that I heard the hammering sounds the men were making and saw my father rushing toward us. "They're almost finished building the platform," he said, urging us to join the festivities.

At exactly ten o'clock, Cino Paci's band came through the cemetery gates with men in uniforms marching behind it. A long line of cars decorated with red, white, and blue streamers followed the band. Then, the mayor's car, which was always the last to arrive, pulled through the gates. When his car stopped, the mayor shook hands with everyone, climbed the stairs to the platform, and talked into a wand that made his voice sound big and booming. He talked and talked, and people clapped and cheered while the band played too loudly.

As soon as the mayor stopped talking, my mom took me by the arm again and led me to the back of the cemetery to stand before my grandmother's grave with its view of the river behind it. There was a picture of my grandmother on her tombstone, one in which she looked both young and old at the same time. Her hair was pulled back, making her eyes appear as large and dark as chestnuts. Her skin was luminous.

Once when it rained, the ink on the picture ran, leaving long dark streaks on her tombstone. To me, it looked as though my grandmother had cried and as though her tears had somehow etched themselves onto the stone.

A CHILD FORGOTTEN

Sometimes on Sundays, my father would take us on trips to the Philadelphia Museum of Art or to the Franklin Institute.

We often picnicked or went for walks along the banks of the Schuylkill River. Once, after we all piled into the back of his car, my father announced we were going to California. He said we were going on vacation, but if we liked it there, "who knows."

My mother, who was sitting in the front seat with the baby on her lap, was smiling, and I knew it was because California was where her youngest sister lived. Her youngest sister, my aunt Maggie, was an army nurse during the war. She was also the only sister my mother never argued with when she talked with her on the telephone.

About an hour after we left, I was still singing "California, Here We Come," although by then I had gone from singing at the top of my lungs to being barely audible, when one of my sisters got carsick. Both Gina and Marie had been taking turns being carsick since we left the house that morning. This time, it was worse, because this time, one of them—I don't remember who—got sick down the back of my father's shirt. Then my father, who always drove with one hand, put both hands on the steering wheel and spun it around until we were going past buildings we had passed before. We were going back to Philadelphia now and our dreams of living in sunny California ended forever.

There were some Sundays, however, when instead of going to Pittston or away on vacation, we would head south to Delaware to visit Aunt Jenny. Aunt Jenny was not really our aunt. We just called her aunt because she was married to Uncle Domenic, who was not our uncle but our father's cousin and the only relative he had in this country.

Domenic was a small, thin man always dressed in a suit. He stood just over five feet and was only a third as wide as Aunt Jenny was. (My father too, was shorter than my mother was, and my cousin said both men were like Napoleon whom I had never met.)

Aunt Jenny had a dress shop downstairs where she made white wedding gowns out of silk and satin material and bridesmaid dresses that hung like rainbows all around the room. Further back in the basement was the wine cellar where my uncle kept barrels full of ruby red and crimson colored wines.

I remember one Sunday when both families sat around a large rectangular table so rickety, it seemed to be fashioned from an old door resting on sawhorses. A white linen cloth covered the table, and platters full of homemade pasta and rich red sauce lay on top of it. On this day everyone seemed to be talking at once, which was in contrast to the way we dined at home where my sisters and I were not allowed to talk at the table.

Uncle Domenic sat at one end of the table and Aunt Jenny at the other. When Uncle Domenic asked for the salt and pepper shakers located at the other end of the table, no one heard him.

"Pass the shakers," Uncle Domenic said again louder. This time Aunt Jenny ignored him.

"Pass the shakers," he said, a third time in his thick, heavily accented voice as Aunt Jenny looked down at him from above her bifocals. She seemed to be giving him a warning. Uncle Domenic ignored it. Instead, he slapped his hands on the table and moved slowly to his feet as a sound came out of him like the growl of an animal emerging from the woods. I sat wide-eyed watching him.

"Sit down, old man," Aunt Jenny said as Uncle Domenic rose to his feet and stepped onto his chair. He climbed onto the table then and walked to the other end to retrieve the shakers. Then, he turned and walked back.

Inside, I felt as though I were cheering for him, urging him to go after what he wanted, even if it were just the shakers. For a moment, I almost forgot where I was and had to put my hand over my mouth to keep the giggles from escaping. Which almost didn't work. When Uncle Domenic jumped back down again, I had to bend over and pretend I was getting something from the floor to keep myself from laughing out loud. Getting up again, I caught a look from my mother that ended my giggles immediately. I sat straight up in my chair then and finished the rest of my dinner in silence.

I liked Aunt Jenny and Uncle Domenic. I liked the way my mom talked to Aunt Jenny, as if they were best friends, and I liked the way they worked together in the kitchen. Aunt Jenny was a lot like my mom. Both women loved to cook, and like my mom, Aunt Jenny often got mad at her husband. But when Aunt Jenny got mad, everybody knew she was mad. When my mom got mad, almost nobody knew because she kept it a secret.

"How did you feel when your mother kept secrets?" Dr. A asked one day several months after therapy began.

I don't know, I thought, irritated today by a process that seemed to be going on forever with no results. Why was he always asking me how I felt when what I felt had happened so long ago? I tried to concentrate, but what I really wanted was to run away from his questions and away from him. I knew, however, that if I wanted to get well, I had to face *it*—whatever *it* was.

Despite my fatigue, I decided to answer. "It made me feel frightened. It made me feel as though her secrets were pockets of air around her—places I was not allowed to enter."

"What kind of places?" he asked.

"Just empty space," I said dismissively, desperately.

"Name it," he said as I sighed. "Give it a name."

"It was a chasm," I said. "It felt like a great big empty chasm between us." And then I asked, "Why are we doing this? Why are we spending so much time on this?"

"You tell me," he said. "Why *are* you doing it?"

I sighed again, then got up and walked to the window. It was a gray day outside, overcast, and cloudy. I watched as several snowflakes drifted aimlessly to the ground. *Why are they there?* I wondered, too tired even to think straight. *Why do they even exist?*

Of course, I knew why I was doing this, why I kept returning week after week. Despite my fatigue, I decided to answer. "I want to understand my life. I want to know what it means and why it happened."

"Good," he said. "then let's continue."

I stood by the window for another minute, watching the snowflakes until I was ready to continue. "My aunt and uncle had two children," I said, still watching the snow. "A boy and a girl, both of whom were older than I was. Or at least I thought there were only two children until the day I found the holy card."

"What holy card?" Dr. A asked as I turned and sat back down on the sofa.

"It was a holy card with the picture of a little boy on it and a black border all around its edges. The boy's first name was Francis, and his last name was the same as my aunt and uncle's. The card said he died when he was five years old. I wondered how he died and I wondered if no one talked about him because no one remembered him."

―――∞∞∞―――

It was late one night two years after the war ended when I heard my mom and dad fighting again. This time it was not about Delores. This time, it was about my father's trip. My sisters and I were peeking out from the bedroom. Daddy's bags were standing by the front door. I could see the old, brown leather suitcases with straps wrapped around each of them.

My dad was keeping a promise he had made to himself to go back to Italy after the war. He wanted to visit the mother who had raised him after his own mother died. He wanted to see his father and his brothers and sisters. He had not been back to Italy in twenty-six years, although he had been sending money to his family all those years, a little every payday. He was proud to be going back and proud he had enough money to do so. He was planning to stay for three months. He even bought one of those moving picture cameras, so he could take pictures of all his relatives and pictures of San Giacomo so that when he left again, he would have something to look at whenever he got homesick.

My mom knew all about the trip, of course. My dad had been planning it for forever. She even agreed to it—reluctantly. She was just upset that he was staying so long. Three months was a long time to be without him. But what she was really mad about, she told him, were those whores, Philomena and her sister Angela, the ones who owned the pizza parlor up the street where they gave him a bon voyage party earlier that night. They always had a thing for him, she said, flirting and swinging their hips in front of him. At the end of the party, they sat on his lap and sang to him about now being the time to say good-bye.

Mommy was angry, but Daddy had to leave because the cabbie kept ringing the doorbell.

"Lil, calm down," he said. "I don't want to leave like this." But my mother kept it up. She wouldn't let go. When my dad opened the door to leave, his head was down and his arms were full of suitcases.

Three weeks later, a telegram arrived for my dad in Italy. It said:

```
RETURN NOW. STOP.
DELORES ELOPED. STOP.
```

The telegram was unsigned. My dad took the next flight home.

Later, my sisters and I watched the home movies he took in Europe. There was one in which he and his brothers and sisters, their arms linked around one another, walked toward the camera. The film was silent, but I could see they were talking. They walked closer and grew bigger until they seemed to walk right through the eye of the person holding the camera.

In the next series of frames, a little boy stooped to examine something on the dirt road beneath his feet. Suddenly, he stood, saw the camera, and then turned and ran away as fast as he could.

"Daddy, why is that little boy running?" Gina asked.

"It was just after the war ended," my dad told her. "And when the little boy saw the camera, he thought it was a machine gun."

THE PANE BETWEEN US

After waiting for years to emulate my sisters, I finally started first grade only to discover I did not want to be in school. Maybe it was because there was something cold and unappealing about the building itself where there were no curtains on the windows and no lacy cloths on the tables. Instead of cotton, there were paper towels and only rubber mats to nap on instead of beneath white cotton sheets and under white, chenille bedspreads with tassels like the one on my bed at home. (Fifteen years later, my young husband, who had been an only child, would describe for me how he had a bedspread identical to the one on my bed. When he was six, he—out of curiosity or out of boredom—used a book of matches to systematically set each tassel on fire until his grandmother discovered what he was up to and put out the fire.)

St. Veronica's had a fire escape that looked like an ugly iron monster growing up from the ground. I had to stand at the top during fire drill, looking down at its steep, narrow steps that made me feel dizzy. I was sure I was about to fall to the ground far below.

Because I hated leaving home, I tried desperately to avoid it. "You have to go to school," my mother told me each morning. "There are no holidays for first graders," she said, "and soon, you'll get used to it." But I didn't get used to it, and as the weather turned colder, I caught a cold that never seemed to leave.

Time passed and still I did not like going to school until I met another girl named Margaret Mary who had long brown hair, which fell in ringlets around her head. People told us we looked like twins. Margaret Mary and I became friends. We spent all our time playing together during recess.

"Margaret Mary, why do you think we have to spend so much time copying letters into our notebooks," I asked her one day after we both missed at double-dutch.

"It has to do with reading," she said. I looked at her suspiciously, wondering how copying could lead to reading. But the very next day, we learned that letters made sounds. "*A* says ah, and *B* says ba." We sang until we made it all the way through the alphabet, repeating this exercise endlessly day after day. When we learned to put the sounds together and sound out words, reading happened.

But Margaret Mary's family moved the summer between first and second grades, and after just a couple of weeks, I decided I had had enough. Because I now knew how to read, I no longer felt as though I had to sit still in class with my hands folded at the edge of the desk and with my eyes always glued to the board. The board was empty and ugly, and I wanted to go outside to play or go home where I could sit quietly with a book opened in front of me.

On our way to school each day, my sisters would pull my arms to make me move faster. When we got to the bridge above the railroad tracks, I would sit on the curb and refuse to budge. "If you pull my arms," I warned them, "my nose will bleed." Then, as if on cue, it began to bleed until Gina took me home and Marie walked on to school alone. This happened repeatedly until, finally, my mom called the doctor who told her to take me to the hospital where I lay in bed with a thin, white sheet covering my nakedness.

My mother stood in a shadow in one corner of the room. Dr. Snyder, our family doctor, stood beside her. Another doctor stood beside me. He drew the sheet to my waist, lifted a round metal-lic disc to my pounding chest and placed its cold surface on top of me.

"Breathe deeply," he said as I held my breath, hoping to dispel the scene in front of me. Everyone was silent as he bent his head to listen. When he murmured "rheumatic fever," his voice sounded like the big booming drum I heard during the Fourth of July parade. Dr. Snyder nodded his head in agreement.

Later, my mom stood in the corner, talking to the doctors who told her I needed to remain in bed for a long time, either at home or in a hospital. "Maybe she can stay with a relative whose children are grown. A relative with a lot of time to take care of her," the strange doctor said to my mother. My mother mentioned Aunt Jenny.

Oh, no. Please don't send me there, I thought to myself. *If I go there, I'll become a child on a holy card, and everyone will forget who I am.* My mother and the doctors talked in whispers. "Okay," Dr. Snyder said, "You can take her home, talk it over with Nick tonight, and let me know tomorrow what you decide." Later, as I lay in bed at Children's Heart Hospital, I waited and wondered if I was now just half a sister to my sisters.

There was a window beside my bed where I watched as the leaves turned from green to gold, then from gold to brown. Some of the leaves became bent and brittle but clung to the branches until the wind began to blow. Then the leaves piled around the bottom of the trees. When the wind blew again, the leaves ran helter-skelter across the hospital grounds and frost began forming in the corners of the window, framing the falling snow.

Before I went to the hospital, I occasionally saw signs nailed to front doors in our neighborhood. Gina told me the signs said "quarantine" and that no visitors were allowed to enter those houses. As I lay in the bed, I wondered if there was a quarantine sign on the front of the hospital because it seemed to take a long time before my parents came to visit.

It was mid-November and snowing the first time I saw my father. It had snowed all night and all day. From my bed, I could hear the nurses talking, saying the roads were too bad for driving. When visiting hours began and ended with no sign of my parents, I burrowed myself deeper under the blankets until one of the nurses came to me and told me to look out the window. I looked and saw my father, standing behind the glass. There was snow falling all around him.

I held my breath, waiting for him to open the window, reach inside, and take me away with him the way he did when I was little. Instead, he looked at me with a look I had never seen before. He closed his eyes, and I closed mine. When I opened them again, he was gone.

A year after I entered the hospital, the doctors said I could leave. At home, my sisters jumped up and down and all over me, so happy were they to see me. Gina was amazed that after a year spent in bed, I remembered how to walk. Of course, I knew how to walk, although even after a year in bed, I still had to stay inside while my sisters played outdoors. But when my father brought home our first black and white television and placed it in the living room, I was happy to watch it from the sofa.

BOYS HAVE SHORT HAIR, GIRLS WEAR DRESSES

A new decade began a few months after I left the hospital and my father moved us from North Philadelphia to West Oak Lane. Although we didn't move to the suburbs, the house my father chose was just two blocks from the city's limit, where Cheltenham and Ogontz Avenues met. The house was a red brick one that stood at the end of a long row of red brick houses.

Instead of concrete, our new house had a lawn that swept around it like the skirt at the bottom of a Christmas tree. My father planted three gardens. When he was done, there were flowers and azalea bushes in the front yard and vegetables growing in the back. In the side yard, he placed a weeping willow tree that hardly wept and a white arbor with red roses, climbing all over it.

There was another weeping willow tree in our neighborhood, and every day on my way to school, I had to pass under it. When it rained, its branches came so close to the ground I was sure they were going to scoop me up and make me disappear forever.

When the first winter storm arrived, it quickly covered the grass and the ground with a layer of snow. Icicles hung from the branches of the trees. From the living room window, I could see the snow-filled streets, which—unlike the streets in our old neighborhood—were silent and hushed even before the snow arrived.

I closed my eyes and imagined hearing the clip-clop of horses, drawing covered carriages the way they did on Christmas cards.

Then from the basement door beside the garage, I watched as snow piled up by inches and then feet. School was cancelled, and my father stayed home from work. I walked upstairs and found the rest of the family collected in the living room, each of us looking around as though not expecting the others to be there. Before long, we gathered around the dining room table, playing rummy and monopoly, while my sisters and I fought over who got the iron, who got the shoe, and who got to be the banker. Feeling protected and safe from the storm, we slipped for a while away from the roles and dramas that kept us apart in our everyday lives.

In the spring, my dad built a flagstone patio outside our front door and covered it with a green canvas awning, then added flagstone steps that lead down the hill and around to the basement floor of our house where he built a rec room.

After he did these things, he worked two jobs and was late getting home every night. During the next ten years, I spent as much time as possible reading a book under the awning or lying beneath the willow tree and looking up at the stars, wishing I could project myself upward to the space between them.

After we moved, we belonged to St. Raymond's Parish, but St. Raymond's had no school. Instead, there were classrooms in the basement of the church and only enough for the first four grades, so my two older sisters had to go to school in a neighboring parish, and I missed them.

My life now revolved around my mother who made me believe she was as strong as an ox although there were moments when she seemed as fragile and delicate as a china cup getting ready to break, and I dared not question or challenge her.

On rainy days, I watched television in the living room, but mostly there was nothing to watch except old movies with Abbott and Costello or Hopalong Cassidy, movies I had seen at the Century when I was little. On Monday nights, I loved to watch *I Love Lucy* because Lucy made me laugh out loud. Even though she was always giving Ricky a bad time, I could tell she really loved him. When Lucy and Desi broke up, I thought the television was going to split in two.

In our new house, the dining room was directly below my bedroom. Every morning, I woke up to the smell of coffee, percolating on the kitchen stove and to the sound of my parents talking quietly together at the dining room table.

After we moved, my mother learned the names of everyone living on our block, the street across from us, and the row of houses that faced our backyard. My mother was friendly and outgoing with neighbors, but at home, she was often withdrawn and angry.

When my mother was angry, she refused to talk to my sisters and me. Instead, she would turn her back and sing one of the hymns she learned as a child. Her favorite hymn to sing was "The Old Rugged Cross." When she got to the chorus, she sang the words as loud as she could, "I will cling to that old rugged cross and exchange it someday for a crown." (I thought she was singing "crayon.")

There were long stretches of time when my mom never smiled, and I thought she was mad at me, but she always told me she was happy when I was good, so I tried to be good all the time. Sometimes, however, I got things wrong, and she would get upset with me. Like that time when we met the neighbor with the new baby.

My mother and I were walking together to the corner store when we met a neighbor named Gwen, who lived three houses down from our house. Gwen had just given birth to an infant she was pushing in a baby carriage. I remember hearing her talk to my mother about her brand-new baby boy.

"Oh, it's a boy," I said.

"Yes," she replied.

"Are you sure?" I asked. "Maybe it's a girl," I said (being partial to girls). "Maybe the doctor made a mistake." Before I realized what was happening, my mother had me by the arm, and we were back inside our living room.

"Why did you ask such a stupid question?" she demanded. "Don't you know the difference between a boy and a girl?"

I looked up at my mom and stammered. I was eight or nine at the time and told her of course I did, although of course I didn't. All I could do at that point was stutter something about boys having short hair and girls wearing dresses. My mother grabbed me by the shoulders and shook me.

"Don't you know boys have," and she used an Italian word and placed her hand between her legs.

What is she talking about? I wondered. *Why did she put her hand there?* Then I remembered something from the previous summer when friends of my parents asked them to be godparents for their newborn baby.

Because the couple lived in Montreal, my dad decided to turn the trip into a vacation. This time we rode all the way to Canada with a minimum of carsickness. At night, we slept in cabins with no electricity and with an overabundance of multi-legged creatures we could just as well have done without, but my sisters and I were excited about being out of the house and on the road together.

My parents' friends lived up on one of the city's many hills where it was so dark at night that when we stepped outside it looked as though a million stars had been tossed across a velvet sky.

I happened to be standing next to the baby one evening when the mother was changing his diaper and that's when I noticed the difference, but having no further use for that information I had simply forgotten it.

When my mother pulled me aside that day, I felt the way I did in school when the nun asked me a question I could not answer because I had not been paying attention. I was embarrassed because I had not remembered the difference, while my mother—I thought—was embarrassed because she did remember the difference.

Before I went into the hospital, I often practiced reading, sitting on my father's lap as he pointed out stories for me to read. After we moved, my father called me only when he saw a story in the newspaper he thought important enough for me to know about, and we would read the *Evening Bulletin* together.

That was how I learned that Josef Stalin was a dictator. On the day of the Russian leader's funeral, my father called me to show me the newspaper stories about Stalin. We read the stories together as my father explained to me that Stalin had been a dictator who had killed too many of his own people.

One day, after reading a story with my father, my mother called me into the kitchen to tell me I was too big to sit on my father's lap. She told me not to do it again. I wondered why my mother told me that and why my father did not tell me himself. Afterward, I felt bad, but I did not understand why I felt bad. Again, I felt as though I had been caught not knowing something I was supposed to know. But there seemed to be more to it than that. There seemed to be something about sitting in my father's lap my mother wanted me to be ashamed of too.

On a June evening in 1953, my father called me to his side to show me a story about Ethel Rosenberg who had been executed earlier that day. "She wasn't guilty," my father said. "She was a scapegoat."

"I don't understand, Daddy. What does scapegoat mean?"

"Scapegoats," he answered, "are people who are blamed for something that is not their fault." My father stopped talking then, but seemed to be searching for something more to say. "Like someone who is born here but raised in a foreign country, and when he speaks, he speaks with an accent." I looked at my father who spoke with an accent and wondered if he was ashamed of himself because of it.

BLINKING LIGHTS AND SHOOTING STARS

My mom had a funny way of looking at me, and whenever she looked at me that way, I thought something was wrong with me. Like maybe my nose was growing crooked or maybe an extra eye had suddenly appeared in the middle of my forehead. But whenever I checked, everything seemed to be right where it was supposed to be.

At St. Raymond's, when a visitor came to our classroom door, it was usually the principal. When we heard a knock, the nun in charge stopped whatever she was doing and walked to the door. The kids would get real quiet then, so they could hear whatever was being said, or they would get real noisy. The difference depended on just how strict that particular nun was and how much homework that noise was going to generate.

In sixth grade (St. Raymond's had built a bigger school by the time I got to fifth grade), our teacher was Sister Marie, who taught us in fourth grade too. In between, Sister Regina, who was new to the school, was our teacher. It was her first year teaching, and we took full advantage of her inexperience. Everyone started behaving poorly. Pandemonium erupted and even the "good" kids started misbehaving. We stopped listening. We called out to one another across the room, and by three o'clock every day, the floor was littered with spitballs.

The following year on the first day of class, Sister Marie assigned us seats alphabetically—boys on the left side of the room, girls on the right. We were excited about being in school as sixth graders. But before we even finished settling ourselves into our new places, Sister got up, came around her desk, and started talking, telling us how Sister Regina had returned to the convent every day after school in tears.

Sister Marie had a special way with words; she spoke them low, so low we had to lean forward (on this occasion, on books that were still piled high on top of our desks) and strain our ears to hear them. Today, when she said the words "in tears," she was almost shouting. "Unlike the Lord," she said, going back to her hoarse whisper, "you were merciless, and you will pay for your sins and insensitivities."

While she was talking, I aligned my head behind the head of the girl, sitting in front of me and peeked around the room. Some of the other girls were wiping tears from their faces with the back of their hands. The boys, who were normally fidgety, were sitting starkly still and silent. Everyone looked guilty. But for me, if there was something I *had* learned in fifth grade (and I had not learned much), it was that chaos came with its own punishment.

By the time Sister was finished, the cloud hanging over our heads was thicker than the mushroom cloud from a nuclear explosion. "I have arranged," she said finally, "for Father to hear your confessions."

At that exact moment, Father came into the classroom. Then, as Sister Marie continued teaching, we had to walk—one at a time—to the back of the room to confess our sins and to receive our penance. Our penance, however, did not end there. For the rest of that school year, Sister Marie dispensed her own form of penance, loading us with homework every chance she got.

On this particular day, Sister turned back from the door of the classroom and called my name. "Antoinette," she said, "You have a visitor." I blinked back tears, embarrassed at being singled out in front of my classmates. I could not imagine who my visitor could be. I went to the door real curious then and felt thunderstruck when I saw my mother, standing there. She extended her hand and gave me the handkerchief I had forgotten that morning.

My mom was always particular about hankies and even gave my sisters and me a box of them every year under the Christmas tree. My mother was especially careful to make sure I always had a hanky because I was so prone to colds, even after leaving the hospital. Of course, I needed that hanky so the sniffles would not end up on the sleeve of my uniform blouse.

That visit from my mom was a real surprise because she had never come to my school before. She didn't drive and must have had to walk all the way just to deliver it. When I saw her there, she almost smiled, and I forgot all about the funny way she looked at me.

After that, I started helping my mother in the kitchen more often. The kitchen was where she liked to spend all of her time, making homemade pasta with meats that melted in your mouth after they had been simmering all day in her rich tomato "gravy." Now I set the table for dinner or helped her with the dishes.

Sometimes while I helped, she told me stories about growing up in Pittston. But my mother's stories were not like the stories my father told at the dinner table. Her stories sounded like secrets she was telling just to me. Sometimes when she told me her stories, she would touch my arm, holding me still until the story ended.

I reached eighth grade in 1955, still feeling as though I were blindfolded and searching for a safe place to fall. My sense of isolation felt bottomless until I discovered I felt comfortable only after I entered St. Raymond's Church. I loved walking into its cool darkness from the bright sunlight outside. I loved sitting in its polished, wooden pews and watching as the sunlight poured through the stained glass windows above them.

The front of the church was divided into three altars with a statue of the Holy Family on the left and a larger than life statue of the Blessed Mother on the right. The concept of a *holy* family felt foreign to me, so I stayed away from that side of the church. Instead, I spent an eternity kneeling in front of the Blessed Mother, asking her to help me feel better around my own mother. Mostly, however, my prayers went unanswered.

I remember walking to church one rainy Saturday in March when I was twelve. The nuns must have liked keeping tabs on us kids seven days a week, because confessions were always held on Saturday afternoons between 3:30 and 4:30. I must have been nervous too, because I was always nervous about going to confession, never certain I could come up with just the right sins to satisfy the priest who was listening to my confession.

I always examined my conscience by going through all the commandments and by looking at what the nuns called the occasions of sin, which included thinking "bad thoughts." Sometimes just hearing the words "bad thoughts" made me start thinking about things I should be avoiding.

I sure had plenty of bad thoughts a year earlier when my mom had to go to the hospital to get our youngest baby sister, Ronnie, and it was taking a long time. Gina was in charge of us whenever my dad wasn't home, but Gina's cooking wasn't nearly as good as my mom's, so right away, I was thinking bad thoughts about that doctor for keeping my mom so long. The good thing about Gina, however, was that she gave me a nickel every day, so I could go to Siggy's drugstore to get a soda.

I would sit at the soda fountain every day after school, reading fan magazines that Siggy let me read for free as long as I didn't wrinkle any pages. I used to sit on one of those red vinyl stools along Siggy's counter, sipping soda, while Johnny worked behind the counter.

Johnny, who was both black and cool long before either word came to mean what they do today, wore his long straight hair combed back in a style he called "processed" with a red bandanna over it. Minus the bandanna, it looked just like the DAs (an acronym that meant duck's ass) all the other boys were wearing.

Whenever I arrived at the drugstore, Johnny was behind the counter, making chocolate egg creams or scooping ice cream into paper cups and topping it with whipped cream, cherries, and syrup. The things Johnny did with that ice cream made him look like a magician.

One day, while Johnny was working, I sat at the counter, reading a fan magazine and sighing every couple of minutes. I must have sighed one too many times, because Johnny, who after putting my five-cent chocolate coke in front of me usually paid no mind to me, walked over and stood in front of me.

"What's up, little one?" he asked. That's when I told him how my entire family had almost made it to California when I was little.

"I wish we had," I said. "Because if we had, I just know I'd be sitting in Schwab's in my best cardigan sweater and pleated skirt waiting to get discovered the same way Lana Turner was."

Johnny laughed. Then he looked at my face and got serious. "Don't you know, little one"—he leaned so close I could smell the bubble gum on his breath—"that some dreams are not meant to come true?" He turned and started walking away. Then he turned around again and looked at me. "And some are," he added with a wink and a smile. I stared at the back of his head for a minute, wondering what Johnny's dreams were before I went back to the *Movieland* magazine, sitting on the counter in front of me.

My mom took nine days to get that baby, and my dad said it was because the doctor told him he had to pick between my mom and the baby. My dad told him that was easy because he already had four perfectly good little girls at home who needed their mother. When my dad told me what the doctor said, I got mad and started getting bad thoughts about that doctor that I could not get rid of until my mom came home again.

As it turned out, that doctor knew nothing. When my mom came home, she brought the new little baby girl with her, although that baby was not much company at first. She would just lie there all day, either sleeping or screaming until someone picked her up. When she screamed like that, her arms and legs would flail so much they made her look like a chicken without its head. I just knew if she didn't get some control over her body pretty soon, she was going to have one heck of a time sitting still all day with her hands folded at the edge of her desk by the time she got to St. Raymond's.

It seemed to take a long time for that baby to lift her head and look around at the rest of us. Now whenever the relatives came over (and there were twice as many relatives after we moved because that's when my dad's side of the family started moving over from Italy), it wasn't just for my mom's good cooking, but to look at that baby and coo over her and say how cute she was.

Sometimes when I went to confession, I could not come up with enough sins to make a good confession, and I had to make up sins to tell the priest. My favorite sin to make up was disobeying my mother, which was not true because in those days I was always too busy trying to make her happy to be disobeying.

"Father," I would tell the priest with my heart pounding, "I took the name of the Lord in vain."

"How many times?" He always insisted on knowing the numbers.

"Three," I would answer because that was my favorite number.

"Anything else?" he would ask as though he was tired and about to yawn widely.

"I disobeyed my mother. Twice," I would add, and even in the darkness of the confessional, I could see him nod.

"And I lied twice," I would tell him, happy now to have some real sins to confess.

Then, I would hear Father sigh as though all the bad things in the world were packed inside him. "For your penance, say three Hail Marys," which was my cue to start saying the Act of Contrition. "O my God I am heartily sorry," I would begin, saying that prayer as fast as I could so I would not forget any of the words. When I finished, Father would say, "*In nomine Patruse et fili e Spiritu Santu,*" and all the other Latin words that felt good, tumbling down on top of me as he gave me his blessing. Afterward, I knelt in a pew and said my penance.

On that particular Saturday, I must have had some really good sins to tell Father because when I finished confessing, I felt good, knowing the Holy Spirit had come to wash all the grayness away from my soul. When I walked through the door of the church, I noticed right away that the rain had stopped, and the sun was shining. As I stood at that door, half inside and half outside, I felt a feeling I had no way of identifying then.

Every spring a carnival came to St. Raymond's. From inside the classrooms, I listened as men with hammers and drills set up the booths. Then, on the second Saturday night in June, I would return to the parking lot outside the church.

Even from a block away, I could see the white lights, surrounding the perimeter of the lot and hear music, blaring from loud speakers set up in each of its corners. I used to walk straight to the middle of the lot, close my eyes, spin around in circles, and then look up at the blinking lights that now looked like shooting stars crisscrossing above me.

Some of the booths sold French fries or funnel cakes while at others men shouted, "Three balls for a quarter. Try your luck." Or they hollered, "Hit three bottles and win a prize." Red-cheeked Kewpie dolls and oversized stuffed animals hung from wires in every booth while red glass plates and goblets lined the shelves and served as consolation prizes.

With a handful of nickels, I walked to the booth with the wheel of fortune on it. The wheel had spaces numbered from one to thirty and corresponding numbers lined a board along the front of the booth. I would put a nickel on one of those numbers, usually the number thirty because I was born on that day in August. If I hesitated before putting my money on the board, the man behind the counter would put his hands into the pockets of his apron and rattle the coins inside. Whether it was out of nervousness or a desire to entice me further, I never knew.

When the wheel started spinning, I would hold my breath as it went around and around, faster and faster while my eyes were glued to it. The excitement, which seemed to be jumping from the wheel directly into my stomach, grew bigger and bigger until I couldn't stand it any longer. Finally, the wheel slowed, then stopped, and I started breathing normally again.

It didn't really seem to matter if I won or lost. I hardly even noticed. I was like Alice, moving toward the looking glass. But unlike Alice, I did not want to go through it. Instead, I wanted to look into it to see myself reflected, to reassure myself that I was real—that I was visible. For a little while, my heart beat so fast while I waited for the wheel to stop that I just knew I was real. But only for a while.

THE TEN-DOLLAR LOAF
OF ITALIAN BREAD

In the mid-fifties, my best friend Jane and I were card-carrying members of the Free Library of Philadelphia whose bookmobile parked itself midway between her house and mine every Friday afternoon after school. I wanted to read all of the books in the bookmobile, starting with authors whose last name began with the letter *A*, but Jane, whose father was dean of the English department at a local university, encouraged me to be more discriminating about the books I read.

Until Jane came along, I had trouble keeping best friends because my mom never liked any of the girls I chose. But since Jane's older sister was my older sister's best friend, I knew that this time I had happened upon just the right person to be my best friend.

Because my mom approved of Jane, I got to spend a lot of time at her house, and it was not long before I noticed the difference between her parents and mine. The first thing I noticed was that Jane didn't seem to have to introduce herself to her mother every time they met and that Jane's mother not only acknowledged her daughter, she often smiled at her (and at me) whenever we entered the room. I don't even have to close my eyes to remember her mother standing over an ironing board with a cigarette in one corner of her mouth and a look of rapt attention on her face as she listened to whatever Jane was saying.

Because of his position at the university, Jane's father seemed aloof and forbidding, but whenever Jane appeared, he gave her his full attention, and to me, he was even more intriguing than her mother was. At home, he spent most of his time sitting in an armchair in the sunroom with two large stereo speakers on either side of him, listening to classical music while an open book sat on his lap. I fell in love with his intellectualism and wanted to grow up to pattern my life to be just like his.

One evening in the spring of '54, my dad had plans to take the entire family to an outdoor concert at the Robin Hood Dell in Fairmount Park. It was getting late, and my sisters and I were all trying to get ready to leave at the same time. In our house when it came to using the bathroom, seniority ruled.

Gina was already out of the bathroom, and Marie was in there with the door locked, so to save time, my mother told me to use the shower in the master bedroom. As I was undressing, I noticed something peculiar in my underwear. When I told my mother, she gave me her strange look, then handed me a pad and told me to wash up quickly.

I did as I was told, all the while wondering how one tiny pad was going to save my life and keep all the liquid inside me from leaking out. As the orchestra played that evening, I sat with my family on the grass outside the amphitheater, keeping my legs close together.

"Gina," I said, rushing into the bedroom the next day after finding her alone. In West Oak Lane, Joanne and Marie shared one bedroom while Gina and I shared another. Because she was older than me, she got to sleep alone on the large double bed while I slept in a smaller one.

Things had gotten difficult between Gina and me recently, having become that way when I discovered she was reading parts of my diary out loud to her best friend. The two of them were laughing so hard while reading it, they didn't notice when I grabbed Gina's homework from the desk where she left it, took my fountain pen, and, shaking it hard, held it above her sheet of loose leaf paper until dark ink spots fell all over it. On the day after our trip to Robin Hood Dell, however, I was willing to forgive her that indiscretion as long as I got some answers.

When I gave her the details, she looked at me strangely. "Don't you know what a period is?"

I looked at her baffled as she threw her hands up in disgust. "Your menstrual period. Weren't you expecting it?" I shook my head. Despite her impatience, Gina gave me the details, telling me I was a woman now. I had been expecting womanhood ever since the day I looked at my chest (after making sure everyone else was out of the bedroom) and noticed it was beginning to bud, but this new development took me by surprise.

"But, Gina, why this?" I asked, finding the whole thing unpleasant and unnecessary.

"I told you. Because you're a woman now" she said, irritated by my questions. "Oh, and by the way, this thing is going to return, month after month, until you reach old age and get ready to croak."

When St. Raymond's built the new school, our class of eighty students was divided into two classrooms. Now Jane and I were separated. We drifted apart; and the twins, Annie and Ellen, became my new best friends.

My mom didn't like the twins much, but by that time, it didn't matter because I was moving toward rebellion. Had I known the direction in which rebellion would take me or had I known that one day it would almost cost me my life, perhaps I would not have found it so enticing. As it was, rebellion was all the rage. After all, it was 1955. James Dean was my idol, and Elvis was just around the corner.

The twins and I discovered boys and Bandstand almost simultaneously. It didn't become American Bandstand until 1957 when Dick Clark took it to Hollywood. Before that, it was just plain old Bandstand and its originator, a man named Bob Horn, broadcast it from an arena in West Philadelphia that he filled with students from local high schools.

In seventh grade, the twins and I would leave school every day as soon as the bell rang and rush home to watch the show. After dinner, we stayed on the telephone, comparing our observations for as long as we could or for as long as our parents allowed, which turned out to be surprisingly long, even in my house.

The teenagers who danced to the music on Bandstand became instant celebrities, and the twins and I took the Broad Street subway one day to center city so we could get their autographs. I really liked a boy on the show named Tommy whom I wanted to see in person. But we couldn't find any celebrities in Philadelphia that day. We were on our way back when I suddenly stopped dead in my tracks at the top of the steps that led to the subway.

"Oh my God," I said, practically screaming at the top of my lungs. "I can't find the twenty-five cents I had for the subway ride home." I continued digging around in my pockets, but it was no use. The money had fallen through a hole in the pocket of my dungarees.

"You're going to have to ask someone for a quarter," Ellen said.

"I can't," I said. I was terrified. I had been taught from an early age not to trust strangers. Two years earlier, when my baby sister turned two, my dad had picked her up, put her on top of the buffet in the dining room, and told her to jump, promising her he would catch her. As she jumped, he moved away, and she fell onto the carpet, unhurt but crying. Then he turned to me and said, "Don't ever trust anyone. Not even your own father." Just the thought of looking a stranger in the eye scared me. The thought of approaching a stranger to ask for money made me feel as though I were blindfolded and trying to find something to grab onto to anchor me in place.

As we passed an old stone building with walls that rose high above street level, Annie told me the building was the Eastern State Penitentiary. My head filled with visions of escaped and crazed inmates running after me. Even more frightening, however, was the thought that I could be stuck in the city indefinitely, especially in light of the fact that we had not asked permission to take the subway and neither of our families knew where we were.

The twins and I stood there for what seemed like hours studying the faces of strangers passing by. "Hurry up," Ellen said as we heard the roar of the train coming from below the grates in the sidewalk. "Pick somebody." Finally, I saw a pleasant looking, heavy set woman who was wearing a dark blouse and a skirt patterned with red roses. She wore a light spring coat over it and a hat with a veil on her head that made her look as though she were on her way to church. She smiled as I approached.

"I've lost my money for the subway," I said, "and if I don't get home soon, my mom will kill me." She laughed at that but opened her purse. I swallowed as my eyes followed her hands deep inside it. From the bottom of the purse she found a quarter and handed it over to me cheerfully. "Thank you," I called to her as the twins and I bounded down the dimly lit steps to the subway and hopped onto the northbound train where I thanked God for her. Without her, I just knew I was going to wind up at the bottom of a ravine somewhere with no identifying marks and no one to claim me.

Because I wanted to show up on Bandstand one day to dance with Tommy, I did a lot of practicing at home with the banister post at the bottom of the stairs. That banister post served as a delightful dancing partner and temporary prince charming until

I could begin to date, which—I knew from listening to the arguments between Gina and my mother—was never going to happen, and, as Gina put it, I was going to wind up a "dried-up prune of an old maid" before my mother relented.

"Your father will kill us all," was what my mother said when I asked her why I was not allowed to date. But I didn't believe that. Not for a minute (although perhaps in light of what happened later I should have). Anyway, the twins and I usually skirted around this issue by going out in large groups of boys and girls so that, technically, I was not breaking the rules.

To me, being a rebel meant dressing like one, but because I had two older sisters, most of my clothes were hand-me-downs. When I was fourteen, however, I found a blouse in the back of their closet I was sure my sisters had never worn and would never be caught dead wearing. It had long sleeves and wide, vertical, neon colored stripes in all the primary colors and must have been truly hideous. But I loved it. Every day after school, I ran into the house, tore off my uniform and wore it over dungarees.

I was wearing that blouse the day my mother handed me a ten-dollar bill and sent me to the bakery for a loaf of bread. I walked into the store, ordered a loaf of Italian bread, put the change into the pocket of my dungarees, and waited for the bread to be sliced. Then I walked back up the street and shivered as I passed William's house.

William was a boy in my class, a skinny, quiet boy, who was also an altar boy. One Sunday morning, when it was hotter in church than it must have been in hell, William fainted right there on the altar in the middle of mass. There he was kneeling on the altar one minute, waiting for the priest to get to the Consecration so he could ring the bell, when he fell straight backward, his head thudding to the ground with the heavy sound of a bowling ball.

In those days, there was no air-conditioning anywhere, except at the movies, where you had to wear a sweater to keep from freezing to death. In addition to the heat, William probably had not eaten breakfast. In the fifties, we were not allowed to eat anything before receiving Holy Communion. Back then, it was not enough to go to confession every Saturday afternoon, we also had to go without eating anything at all from Saturday night until after mass on Sunday.

The nine o'clock mass was the children's mass, and we had to sit in pews with our classmates and with the nun who was our teacher, who you just knew was mentally taking attendance and watching us like a hawk. God forbid you forgot yourself for one moment and did any fidgeting in church. If you did, you would find Sister's finger, poking itself into your back.

Going to mass and receiving communion were mandatory. If you missed mass you had to have a note from your parents with a good reason in it, like you had to run to the hospital before nine o'clock on a Sunday morning to visit your great Aunt Mary who was lying on her deathbed and was expected to be dead before mass began.

If you didn't walk to the altar to receive communion, everyone assumed you had committed a mortal sin since your last confession on Saturday afternoon, and you were going straight to hell if you died before you could get to confession the following week.

Walking back up the street, I must have been remembering how William had fainted in church that Sunday. I must have been swinging that loaf of bread as I passed William's house, trying not to think about how fainting had made his head seem empty and vacant because when I got home, I reached into my pocket for the change but only the coins were there. The five-dollar bill and four ones I had so carefully folded into eighths and put into my pocket were gone.

My mom yelled and sent me right past William's house again to look for that money, but it was gone. As my mother yelled, I felt small and invisible and knew that not even a multicolored shirt was going to be enough to make me feel real.

FROM JEKYLL TO HYDE

The Sisters of Mercy must have had a shortage of nuns that year because when I finally got to eighth grade, we had the same nun we had in seventh grade. By eighth grade, we were a difficult group of more than forty classmates and becoming the oldest kids in the school was going to make us even harder to handle.

Sister Francis had already demonstrated she knew how to control us, although she lost my vote the day she took a ruler to the knuckles of one of the twins. I had never before seen anyone struck, and in my eyes, Sister became a bully that day.

Sister Francis was a tall, big-boned woman with a large hooked nose and a perennially red complexion. Behind her back, where most things happened—or so we believed—we called her "the Indian."

One day early in the school year, I found myself engaged in an activity I had never tried before. I was flirting with one of the boys. After a couple of minutes of this, Sister came tearing down the aisle so quickly her rosary and black veil were almost left behind. She towered above me even before the last word was out of my mouth.

"Young lady, I will see you after school," she decreed. I had never been in trouble before, and her words slapped me like the sound of her ruler. It was only 1:30, and I had to pass the next two hours in utter mortification. At 3:20, I prayed Sister had forgotten me, but one look from her convinced me otherwise. She led me to the back of the classroom and into the cloakroom.

"What happened in class?" she questioned with the same look the judges of the Inquisition must have given Galileo. Everyone knew that if you lied to a nun, you would go straight to hell, so I was trapped. I had to admit to flirting.

"But what was it he said to you?" she demanded.

When I told her, she reeled back a full one hundred and eighty degrees and, if possible, turned an even deeper shade of red than usual.

"Where did you learn that word?" she demanded.

"What word?" I asked.

"That word, the bad word," she spat out at me.

I was baffled. Bad word? What bad word? I didn't even know words *could* be bad. What word was she talking about anyway? I went through the entire sentence in my mind. *It must be that one*, I thought. It's the only one I had never heard before.

"Do you mean *fuck*?" I asked, looking directly at her.

When I got home, my sister Marie was the only one there, except for my mother. When I told Marie what happened and asked her what the word meant, her reaction was even stranger than the nun's was. Marie cried.

I don't know why Marie cried that day, but it was a reaction that stuck with me, like an alarm going off in my head. For years, I had suspected there was something not quite right about my mother, and now, I began to suspect that whatever it was, it had gotten to my older sister and was heading straight for me too.

I graduated from eighth grade that year and bought my first record. It was Elvis's "I Want You, I Need You, I Love You." I played it over and over again until the hole in the middle got too large and the needle skipped to the end every time I tried to play it. But that summer before high school, the world seemed full of promise and ready to open up in front of me. Then, just weeks into my freshman year, a death in the family brought those good feelings to a standstill.

Aunt Nancy was my mother's younger sister and at forty-one, just a year younger than my mother was. My aunt had married a fellow Pittstonian named Cataldo, whom—for some reason—we called Uncle Sam. The couple had three children—Cataldo Jr., whom we called Sonny, and his brothers Johnny and Salvatore. Aunt Nancy had always wanted a daughter but had to settle instead for a collection of dolls.

According to my mother, Uncle Sam spoiled my aunt, giving her everything she ever wanted. Less than a year before her death, my aunt and uncle moved from North Philly into a new house not far from ours. It was near the Sears store at Adams Avenue and Roosevelt Boulevard, and I was with my parents the first time they went to visit Aunt Nancy there.

She took us on the grand tour of the house, which she had decorated with brand-new furniture and the dolls she had been collecting since she realized she was never going to have a daughter of her own. The most beautiful doll I ever saw was dressed all in lavender, which was my aunt's favorite color. The doll had a lavender gown that was spread out all around her and displayed on the center of my aunt's bed in the master bedroom.

I was in the kitchen with my mother and aunt when I heard my aunt complain about not being able to afford new clothes. "It's been forever since I've bought anything new," she told my mother.

To which my mother replied, "Look around you, Nancy. You just bought a house and filled it with new furniture."

Aunt Nancy laughed, but my mother would not relent. She believed that as the oldest, her sisters had never given her the respect she deserved and had never listened to her.

Not long after, I heard my mother arguing with Aunt Nancy on the phone. This time, it must have been serious because I do not remember anyone talking to or about Aunt Nancy for weeks afterward. I know my mother was still mad at Aunt Nancy when news of the accident got to her.

As soon as word reached Philadelphia, my mother called Aunt Maggie in California. Then she, her younger sister Clara, and her older brother Nicky boarded a train to North Carolina. Later, we were to learn that my mother remained stoic, never crying during the entire week she was there at her sister's bedside, not even after her sister died.

Back home, we were slowly learning the details of the accident, which occurred while the family was en route to see Sonny, who had just joined the Marine Corps and was stationed at Camp Lejeune. Their car had just crossed into North Carolina along a rural stretch of US-1, (I-95 had not yet been completed) when the driver of a tractor-trailer went through a stop sign and slammed into their car.

All of the family members inside the car were seriously injured. My aunt, who had been seated in the front passenger seat, went through the windshield, and my cousin Johnny's right ear was "hanging by a thread." An ambulance rushed the family to a nearby hospital.

At her viewing, Aunt Nancy was dressed in a lavender gown and lavender shoes. I remember seeing my uncle, his face bruised and battered while his hands moved often to his ribcage. Thick layers of gauze covered Johnny's ear, and Sal sat off to one side looking wounded and dazed. The entire family looked wounded, except for Sonny, who looked devastated.

I remember hearing some whispering that night because Sonny's girlfriend, who had also been in the car but not injured, was dressed in a blouse cut lower than most of the women in the family thought necessary. During the entire viewing, my mother remained stoic and subdued.

The next day after Requiem Mass, we went to the cemetery where Aunt Nancy's lavender casket sat on ropes suspended above the newly opened earth. The priest was praying, sprinkling holy water as we stood at the gravesite. When he finished, we took turns placing flowers on top of the casket. I was standing beside and slightly behind my parents as I watched the casket being lowered into the ground. Suddenly, I heard someone scream. I stood on tiptoe and looked in the direction of the screaming, but it took a long time before my brain made sense of what I was seeing.

Finally, I realized Sonny was trying to throw himself onto his mother's casket. People were rushing toward him, screaming, "No, Sonny, don't do it," and "Please, Sonny, stop." Some of the men were holding him back by the arms, pulling him away from the grave. At that moment, my mother's body seemed to convulse and erupt into one loud, agonizing scream.

I started to move toward her, then stopped as my father, who was closer, got there before me. He put his arm around her and started crying too. I stood there transfixed, watching my parents reflect one another's grief. Even then, I knew that in a relationship, any relationship, the two people involved acted as a mirror for one another. I knew, too, that I had no such mirror to look into.

I felt different after the funeral, as though there was less of me than there was before. Even just thinking about my aunt's death made me feel smaller, like Alice again, except that I wasn't lost in a wonderland, but in a place where I was all alone and blindfolded.

Looking back later, I wondered if it was watching my parents come together and close ranks that made me feel so isolated and alone. But whatever the reason, for the next six years, I have no memories of any interactions with any member of my family.

—∞—

"You have no memories at all?" Dr. A asked. Was I imagining it, or did he actually sound incredulous?

"None."

"Why do you think that is?"

"I don't know."

"Well," he said slowly while looking at me intently, "why not think about it? Come up with something. What do you think made you feel that way?"

I closed my eyes, mostly to humor him, but then something happened. A snapshot, a brief moment returned to me from the past. I opened my eyes again, feeling somewhat incredulous myself. "Dr. A, do you know what I saw just now when I closed my eyes?" I asked as I sat up straighter and inched closer to the edge of my seat.

"What did you see?"

I smiled a little, knowing that what I was about to say was going to sound strange. "I saw the train set we used to have under our Christmas tree when I was little. My father bought it and brought it home when I was maybe ten or eleven. When he showed it to me, I could tell that the set made him happy, like it was something he had always wanted himself.

"But I was bored with it almost from the beginning. It just went around and around in circles until finally the engine jumped the track and all the cars went tumbling down behind it," I said, and then I went silent, remembering how all the wheels kept on turning furiously even though the cars were lying on their sides.

"What happened then?" Dr. A asked, bringing me back to the present.

"I picked up two of the cars," I said. "One in each hand and moved them closer together to connect them. Before I could do anything, they jumped back together. They just kind of jumped back together magnetically. And I heard a click. It was that simple."

"What was that simple?"

"The connection they made. It was like…just like—"

"Like the connection your parents made when they came together at the funeral?"

I looked at him, wondering how he knew what I was thinking. "Yes," I answered.

"And?"

"And…and." I stammered. "It was simple. It was so simple," I said, still mystified.

"But?"

I held my breath for a moment. Then as I spoke, I felt as though all the air was rushing out of my body and the words went tumbling out behind it. "But I couldn't do that," I said. "I couldn't make it happen. Not with my parents. Not with anyone. I couldn't do it then, and I cannot do it now."

Six years later in the spring of 1962, both Marie and I were students at Temple University's main campus on north Broad Street in Philadelphia. After twelve years of Catholic school, I fell in love with the intellectual freedom there and wanted to continue to take courses and studying until I learned "all the answers to all the questions."

Marie had other desires, however. Much more ambitious than I was, she wanted to become a doctor. After learning that Temple had a campus in Rome, she decided to spend a semester abroad.

In the meantime, I was working as a waitress at a Horn & Hardart restaurant not far from home. It was a large restaurant with at least a dozen women working at the same time. All the waitresses were white, while all the kitchen help was black, and

I couldn't help noticing that even high school girls were treated with more respect than the people working in the kitchen.

There was a boy there named Philip, who worked the night shift and ran the dishwasher. It was a huge dishwasher, running the length of an entire room, and Philip ran it all night, every night. Philip was a small, thin boy, and at five feet four, he was just two inches taller than I was. He had skin as black and as glowing as the sky at midnight.

He was also the quietest person I had ever met. He was even quieter than I was, and whenever I asked him a question, he would give me only one-word answers. When I brought this to his attention, he just smiled as though he were pleased I'd noticed, but said nothing. After that, it became a kind of game between us. I would ask him things I knew needed more than one word to answer. He would smile and give me his one-word answer, and I would laugh and walk away.

Another man in the kitchen, Marcus, was a kind of guru there. Everyone respected his opinion, even the management. Once when I asked him why people were not as happy as I thought they should be, he told me it was because people were afraid of happiness. He said they were afraid of the price they would have to pay for it.

And then, there was Lawrence, a sweet, sensitive boy with honey-colored skin and beautiful dark eyes that looked out at the world as though they could not quite believe what they were seeing. He and I became friends and spent hours together, talking. Sometimes I would walk with him to the bus stop, which was on my way home. We even kissed, often and long.

Of course, it didn't take long for my father to hear about it. Furious, he forbade me to see him again. But when Lawrence enlisted in the air force and went away for training, we stayed in touch by mail.

I was upstairs in my bedroom writing a letter to Lawrence one day while my parents were downstairs entertaining friends.

When I finished the letter, I walked downstairs, stopped to greet my parents' guests, and then walked across the street to mail the letter. When the guests left, my father called me downstairs, demanding to know why I went across the street to the mailbox.

Growing up, my father had always reminded me of Spencer Tracy, and I guess what I wanted at that moment was Spencer Tracy in *Guess Who's Coming to Dinner* (even though the movie was yet to be made.) Instead, I got Tracy from one of my dad's favorite movies *Jekyll and Hyde*. When I told him the letter was for Lawrence, his face froze, then contorted with rage and anger.

He lunged forward, placing his hands around my throat. He looked directly at me and started choking me, all the while screaming that he was going to kill me. But I wasn't listening to his words. I was stunned, frozen with fear, and close to passing out before Gina and my mother pulled him away. I fell to the floor, backed away from them, and then got up and ran back up the stairs.

In my room, I stood trembling. Holding on to the bedpost, I braced myself. I stayed in my room a long time, thinking about the stories my father told me when I was growing up. After moving to this country, my father had felt different, sometimes ostracized, because his accent made him feel different. That night, I wondered why my father could not expand those feelings to include people whose skin color was different from his.

I remembered my father's love for this country, for a country, which seemingly took no pride in him. It was easy to see how much he loved living here, but for my father and perhaps for his entire generation, love was not a source of strength, but a sign of weakness. I wondered then if in my father's mind love and shame were all mixed up together. *Was that it? Was my father ashamed of me? Why was it,* I wondered, *that my father did not know that the really shameful people were the ones who tried to shame others?*

I cried myself to sleep that night, and by morning, I knew I had to leave. I could no longer live in my father's house. I no longer wanted to live in my father's house. All of my life, he had been teaching me to be afraid of strangers. Now, I was afraid of him. I knew I had to leave as quickly as possible.

But something else happened before I could act on that decision.

THERAPY

You think you know what to look for in life...You think your childhood teaches you all the traps you need to worry about. But that's not how it works. Pain doesn't travel in straight lines. It circles back around and comes up behind you. It's the circles that kill you.

—Pat Conroy

TEN PERFECT FINGERS
AND TEN PERFECT TOES

"This isn't my first time," I said to Dr. A one day about a year after we began. I was standing by the window, looking out at the sun-drenched street and the fall colors on the trees outside.

"Your first time at what?" he asked.

"At seeing a therapist," I said, turning to look at him. "When I was young, my mother took me to see a psychiatrist."

Dr. A put his hands together and steepled his fingers. "Why did your mother take you there?"

"She took me there because I told her I wanted to leave home. It was 1962, and in those days, girls didn't leave home until they were married."

"What happened when you went to see him?"

"I only went once," I said as I walked back to the sofa and sat down. "It was right after my sister had a nervous breakdown. That's what they called it in those days," I said, wincing. "A nervous breakdown."

"Which sister?"

"Marie," I told him as I picked up the strap from my shoulder bag and began playing with it nervously. "She was hospitalized because of it, and so, I only went once to talk to him. I think my mom figured he'd tell me I was crazy, especially in light of what had happened to Marie." I said, twisting the strap into knots.

"What happened to Marie?" he asked.

"That summer while Marie was in Europe, we received a call in the middle of the night. The voice on the other end told my father Marie had gone missing from her dorm. When the police located her, she was found wandering around the streets of Rome, lost and disoriented. She was speaking incoherently and kept telling the police she had to go to the Vatican to meet with the Pope. The police took her to a psychiatric hospital in Rome.

"On the phone, they told my dad someone had to go to Rome to bring her back, but my father wouldn't go. He said it was because he had to work, but I did not believe him. I knew he was afraid of flying. He had only flown once, after receiving the telegram about Delores after the war, and he hated it."

"So your mother went?" Dr. A asked.

"No. My youngest sister was still in grade school, and my mother said she couldn't leave her. Instead," I said, tossing the strap onto the cushion beside me, "they sent Gina who, at twenty-three, had to deal with the doctors, the hospital, college administrators, and the police. After Marie was released from the hospital, she and Gina went to San Giacomo, so Marie could rest. When they finally returned to the States, Marie was hospitalized again. My mom must have been good at that."

"At what?" he asked.

"At putting people into the hospital," I said, looking at him and then away from him again. "Anyway, that was when my mom took me to see my sister's psychiatrist. She took me to a place called Dufur. It's called something else now. Horsham Clinic, I think.

"To get to the hospital during the day while my father was working, my mother used to take the trolley to the end of the line, then walk the two or three miles to the hospital." Dr. A raised his eyebrows but said nothing.

"I remember the day I was taken there. I remember being inside my father's car as we turned into the driveway. Dufur had a long driveway with tall, old trees stretched along each side of it. I remember how we inched up that driveway and how the trees that lined it reminded me of Twelve Oaks in the movie *Gone with the Wind*," I said as I glanced outside Dr. A's window.

"The landscape around the hospital was so beautiful that for a moment I wondered how bad such a place could be, but then I remembered why my sister was there. I was worried because I was being taken there also. I knew that while my sister was there, they were giving her electric shock treatments. I remembered seeing Marie after one of these treatments. She seemed so…so." I hesitated, and then I was silent.

"What?" he asked, leaning closer. "How did she seem to you?"

"Empty. Vacant. As though she were being drugged," I said. We were both silent for a moment before I continued. "When I went to see the doctor, I think my mom was expecting him to tell me to stay home."

And he didn't?"

I shook my head. "He told me to run. He told me to run like hell. He didn't use those words, of course, but it didn't matter. I got the point." I took a deep breath. "When I told my mother what he said, she didn't believe me. After all, she was paying him and was counting on him to support her."

"Why do you think he told you to run?" Dr. A asked.

I shook my head. "I'm not sure," I said, "but I told him what it was like living at home. I told him that even at twenty-one, I was not allowed to date. That was not so bad when I was still in an all girls' high school, but by the time I got to Temple, I felt differently. I felt so intellectually free. I felt as though I had been released from shackles. I wanted to explore and enjoy my freedom, intellectually and otherwise."

Dr. A was silent again for a moment, and then he asked, "When Marie got sick, did anyone tell you what happened?"

"When he got the phone call, my dad said Marie was in the middle of taking finals. She was in a foreign country and the pressure was just too much for her. But later my mother pulled me aside to tell me 'what really happened to Marie.'"

"Your mother had a different version?"

"Yes," I said, looking down at my hands in my lap.

"What was it?"

"She said..." I stopped, not sure I could continue. When I started again, I spoke the words quickly as though that could change what I was about to say. "She told me Marie had a nervous breakdown because a boy 'exposed himself to her.'" I leaned forward then and raised one knee as though trying to protect my stomach.

"Dr. A," I said, looking up at him. "I was twenty-one, still living at home and still very ignorant about sex, but even I knew that mere exposure to a boy was not likely to cause a nervous breakdown. When my mother said that, I blanched. I felt as though all the blood inside me stopped flowing and everything outside me turned to ice."

"Did you ask your mother to explain?"

"No," I answered, shaking my head. "At that point, her lips were sealed. She may as well have sewn them together. She was not about to answer any questions. She simply took her hand away from my arm, ending the conversation. Dr. A," I said, looking directly at him again, "sometimes, I think my mother's emotional growth was interrupted when she was sixteen, and her mother died."

It was 1931, and the country was in the grip of the Great Depression. While my grandfather worked in the coal mines, my grandmother and my mother ran the candy store in the basement of their home on Drummond Street in Pittston. My mother had been working alongside her mother ever since she completed her schooling at the end of fourth grade. Altogether, there were five children in the household—Uncle Nicky, who was the oldest; my mother Lillian, who had been born in 1914; and her three younger sisters, Nancy, Clara, and the youngest, Margaret.

My parents met in 1930 when my mother was sixteen and my father came into the candy store after work to buy a cigar and some Mary Janes. At first, my mom didn't like my dad. Whenever he came into the store after that, she would run into the house to avoid him. But my grandmother liked him and encouraged my mother to talk with him. Gradually, she came around, and in time, the two became engaged.

When my mother's youngest sister Margaret was born back in 1918, the doctor told Angelina not to get pregnant again because she had diabetes and because he believed another pregnancy would kill her. Thirteen years later, when she learned she was pregnant again, she was determined not to let the doctor find out about it.

In late May, however, she caught a cold severe enough to keep her in bed. Unable to shake the symptoms, she sent my mother for the doctor. Before he arrived, Angelina put several heavy blankets on top of herself to camouflage her pregnancy. The doctor arrived and to her great relief never looked under the blankets. He wrote a prescription and told her to remain in bed until she felt better.

My grandmother's stomach began cramping almost immediately after taking the pills. My mother ran for the midwife, but my grandmother miscarried before they returned. The fetus, my mother said, was a fully developed baby boy with "ten perfect fingers and ten perfect toes." She knew this because she later found it wrapped in a blanket and hidden under the bed.

In the meantime, the after-birth remained inside my grandmother's womb. Despite her best efforts, the midwife was unable to help. My grandmother developed a fever and an infection that my mother called gangrene poisoning, which today would be called septicemia.

When my grandfather came home and heard what happened, he became so enraged with the doctor for prescribing the medicine, he refused to allow him back inside the house. Furthermore, he refused all medical treatment for his wife and would not allow her to be taken to the hospital. The infection inside my grandmother worsened.

By the time he returned from work the following day, his wife was so delirious he finally relented and called an ambulance. Angelina was rushed to the hospital where, according to my mother, she died on the operating table. However, according to the newspaper story my mother kept in her scrapbook, Angelina was admitted to Pittston Hospital on May 29 "where her condition became steadily worse."

Angelina, who had been born on April 1, 1890, died on June 8, 1931. (Years later, it was my mother who underscored for me that my oldest daughter was born on April 1 and that my youngest was born on June 8.)

WHY MY MOTHER WAS ANGRY

"Dr. A, when I was a growing up, my mother told me that story so many times that when I told it to you, I felt as though I were telling it word for word the way she told it to me. Whenever she told it, she put her hand on my arm and kept her voice so low it sounded almost conspiratorial."

"Why do you think your mother put her hand on your arm?"

"I always believed my mother was angry with my grandfather and that she blamed him for what happened. When my mother put her hand on my arm, I thought she wanted… This may sound strange, but sometimes, I thought my mother wanted me to get even for her. She wanted me to be angry too."

"With her father?"

"No," I said, "with mine. You see, all the time I was growing up, there seemed to be an undercurrent of anger in our house; there were battles between my mother and my sisters and at times between my mother and my father. Even though my mother kept silent, I knew when she was angry, and I always aligned myself with her."

"Why was your mother angry with your father?"

"After my grandmother died, she was forced by my grandfather to break her engagement to my father. As the oldest, she had to stay home and do the cooking, the cleaning, and help out with her younger sisters, while my grandfather, who was despondent after losing his wife, began frequenting taverns and staying out late.

My father waited as long as he could, then married another woman named Vera, who had been a friend of my mother's. My father and Vera had a child together, a daughter named—"

"Delores?"

"Yes. Vera, however, was unfaithful (which is definitely not the word my mother used to describe her), and my father finally divorced her to marry my mother. Dr. A, she married him, but I don't believe she ever forgave him." Dr. A looked at me silently.

"In 1987," I continued, "when my father was dying, he turned to my mother and said, 'I love you, Lil.' And mother responded, 'Then why did you marry Vera first?'"

"She held that grudge all those years?" he asked, sounding incredulous.

"Yes," I whispered.

"And when your mother wanted you to be angry with your father, were you?'

"No, not until Marie got sick."

"You blamed it on your father?"

"No," I answered, my voice rising now. "But someone had to go to Europe to bring her back, and my father wouldn't get on a plane and that's when I got angry. I was so angry," I said, feeling the anger rising inside me again.

"Why? Why were you angry?"

"Because she was sick and alone," I said, wanting to scream.

"And?"

"And because he was supposed to rescue her," I answered, pushing the words toward him to end this conversation.

But Dr. A wouldn't relent. "And?" he said, his voice rising.

"He was supposed to rescue her, and he was supposed to rescue me," I screamed. There I'd said it. It was finally out and on the table.

But Dr. A wasn't finished. "When?" he asked, his voice lowered now, almost to a whisper. "When was he supposed to rescue you?"

I wanted to get up. I wanted to run, but I couldn't. I couldn't move. I couldn't breathe. I wouldn't breathe again until I told him. "When my mother sent me away."

Dr. A leaned back and sighed. "When? When did your mother send you away?"

"When I went to the hospital," I told him, crying now. "The doctor told my mother to talk it over with my dad, but she didn't. When he came home, I heard her tell him I *had* to go to the hospital."

When my mother came to live with me at my daughter's house in 1999, I did not recognize her, so different was she from the woman I remembered, from the woman I thought I remembered. In those days, before therapy, I believed the only reason I left home in 1963 was because of what had happened with my father.

My mother was in her mid-eighties by then, and her hair had gone from gray to white. She still wore an apron over her dresses, and although she had a whole closet full of clothes, she seemed to enjoy wearing the same two dresses alternately. Right away, I began noticing things I had not noticed as a child. Like the fact that she liked to play games. She had a dozen different ways of circumventing everything, and she enjoyed doing things "out of spite."

When my father died in 1987, my mother was living with my youngest sister, Ronnie, but after a while, she decided to move. She left my sister's house and found an apartment. One of my aunts also lived in that building. I believe my mother expected her sister to include her in the social circles there, but her sister snubbed her. Because of this and because she was getting older, my mother became more reclusive.

Sometimes when I called the apartment, she would not answer the phone. I became so concerned when I could not get in touch with her that one day I asked my daughter to go with me to see if she was all right. When I got there, I used my key to enter the apartment and found my mother sitting alone in the dark, staring at a television that was not turned on.

After this happened a couple of times, my daughter Jessi and I decided to ask her if she wanted to move in with us. She agreed, or at least I thought she did until I later learned she told one of my sisters that Jessi and I had kidnapped her.

Jessi has four children and the two youngest, Brian and Victoria, used to come downstairs to the apartment every day after school for something to eat, and I would give them something to hold them over until dinnertime. One day after they left, my mother turned to me and said, "You love them too much. You spoil them."

I was flabbergasted. "What?" I asked.

"You love them too much and you spoil them," she repeated.

"Love can't spoil them," I said.

"Yes, it can," she insisted.

"No, you can't spoil anyone with love," I said, wondering why she thought there were limits on love. Why did she pull back? Did she believe love was a source of power, a way of controlling behavior?

What upset me the most, however, was the way she treated my granddaughter Victoria. She seemed to enjoy baiting her. Her relationship with Tori reminded me of the way she related to Gina when we were young. My mother would bait Gina, and Gina always took the bait. She would talk back and the two of them would wind up in an argument. So Gina was always in trouble with my mom. But Tori was only seven and would never have dreamed of talking back, which only made my mother angrier. It seemed as though my mom was trying to groom Tori to be like Gina, or like Delores.

Once, my mother told me a story about something that had happened just after she and my dad were married. She said there was a pool hall across the street from where they were living on Reese Street, and she felt he was spending too much time there.

He had keys to the pool hall, and one night while he was sleeping, she took the keys off his dresser and went across the street. After letting herself in, she used a razor she had taken from home and ripped the green felt on the tables to shreds. She said he suspected she was the one who had damaged the tables, but she never admitted it. I shivered when she told me that story, especially since she seemed so delighted in having gotten away with what she had done.

One morning after she moved in with me, I became so frustrated with her that when I went into the bathroom to brush my teeth, I completely lost it. Suddenly I realized not only had I been beating the tube of toothpaste against the sink, but now the toothpaste was everywhere—on the sink, the mirrors, the walls, and even on the ceiling.

When my mother moved in with me, I thought I was offering her peace of mind. But she did not seem to want that. It did not take long for depression to set in. I knew what depression felt like. I had felt it before, back in 1975 after Nathan and I separated.

When I woke up in the morning, I felt as though there was a dark, heavy cloak on top of me. One that I could not remove. My eyes, too, seemed to be covered with a veil through which I could see nothing but sorrow and sadness.

In addition, I was beginning to feel overwhelmingly lonely. To alleviate the stress, I began taking long walks in the park. There was something wonderful about being outdoors. Nature, I discovered, had its own melody, and as I walked, I realized there was cadence even in silence.

One night in late January of 2001, when there was too much snow on the ground and in the park and the sidewalks were too iced over for walking, I went outside into the cold night to look at the dozens of stars that were framed within the exterior walls of our house. It was much too cold to go any further, but I felt reassured just seeing the stars hanging where they should be, hanging where I knew they would be the following night. The next day, the twentieth, four more inches of snow were expected, so I decided to stay indoors and watch the inauguration.

The only falling snow I saw that day was on television in Washington, DC. I watched, delighted, as the president leaving office (Clinton) did everything he could but chain himself to his desk. It was obvious he had loved his job. *We should all be that lucky*, I thought not realizing I would soon have a job that would make me feel exactly the same way.

As Chief Justice Rehnquist administered the oath to the new president, the heavy snowfall became an incredible backdrop. It was snowing so much I could barely make out the outline of the Capitol building. "I, George W. Bush, do solemnly swear," I heard, completely unaware that at that moment something dark and tragic was happening inside my mother's mind.

On a day late in January, I got up early and left the house for a visit with my daughter Cindi, who was living in neighboring Bucks County. The weather had warmed up a little by then, and as I pulled out of the driveway, I noticed that the snowman my grandchildren had built was but a skeleton of what he once had been. I stayed with my infant grandson, while my daughter went to a meeting with the teacher of her daughter Jacquelyn. When Cindi returned, we sat talking over coffee until late morning.

I was almost home, sitting at the light in front of the old inn on Jarrettown Road when my cell phone rang. I had left the house so early that morning that my mom was still asleep, but I had asked my grandsons, Robby and Michael, to check in on her. The call was from my daughter who said my mom was acting strangely.

When I got home, my mother did not seem to know who I was. What was worse, she did not seem to know who *she* was. I asked her how she was, and she said, "Fine." Then I asked if she was feeling okay, and she said, "No." She was having trouble keeping her balance. Jessi and I got her into the car and took her to our family doctor in Jenkintown, who in turn, called an ambulance and had her taken directly to the ER.

I was frightened by then, frightened for my mother and frightened for the infant I'd been holding hours earlier. Did my mother have something contagious? I worried, and if she did, had I infected Rory? As the doctors began a battery of tests, I called my sisters to tell them what was happening. When the tests were completed, the doctors told us she had Alzheimer's disease.

I spent that first night with her in the ER but went home to sleep the following night. When I returned to the hospital the next morning, the nurses said she had a difficult night. They said she had gotten out of bed and tried to walk out of the hospital—naked. I couldn't believe my mother had done that. It did not sound like something my mother would do. The nurses said she was being restrained, which I learned meant she was strapped to the bed. I spent the remaining days and nights with her at the hospital.

After my mother was diagnosed with Alzheimer's, I wondered if the behavior she showed after moving in with me was really hers or if it had been a result of the disease. I went into mourning then, realizing the mother I had known was lost somewhere deep inside herself. Later, when her death was imminent, I thought I was prepared, but I wasn't.

DR. PHIL AND CHOPRA

Back in 1963, after Gina and Marie came back from Europe, I completed a semester at Temple and made plans to leave home. I quit school and took a job in center city Philadelphia working for an insurance company in a building diagonally across the street from Independence Hall. The apartment I found was just a train ride away from work. It was located at the intersection of Fortieth and Chestnut Streets in a building that has since been torn down, but I liked it because it was close to the University of Pennsylvania and because the rent was only fifteen dollars a week, cheap even by 1963's standards.

Knowing my parents would try to stop me, I did not tell them I was leaving. Instead, I took my clothes a few at a time in brown paper bags, and when I was ready, I left a note, telling them I had found an apartment but not telling them where it was.

I called home at the end of the first week to tell my mother I was all right. Before hanging up, she said something to let me know she knew exactly where I was. When I asked how she knew, she said she had hired a private detective to follow me from work. Years later, however, she said she cried in front of the mailman until he agreed to give her the information from my change of address card. I never knew which story was true.

It was in the kitchen of that apartment that I finally learned about sex. The details came from my friend, Bernice, who was four years younger than I was, and whose mother was a nurse who had told her about sex years earlier. *He puts what, where?* was what I was thinking when she told me.

Bernice said she was able to verify the details herself recently while she and her boyfriend were making out. She said she handed him a tape measure and sent him into the bathroom to measure his erection and to report back to her how much larger his penis was than it had been before they started.

It was not until the end of the year that I was able to verify the facts for myself.

It was November 23, 1963, and news of the Kennedy assassination one day earlier had exploded inside my head and sent me reeling. The news made me feel like a roly-poly toy, ready to teeter and fall at the slightest touch. Like the toy, I felt as though I had no legs to propel me forward.

I was working part time and once again enrolled full time at Temple. Knowing I would probably not have enough money for another semester, I was enjoying every minute of it. I spent all of my free time in either the Sullivan Library or Mitten Hall, which is now an administration building. In those days, however, it was a gathering place for students with its large comfortable sofas and chairs tucked into its nooks and crannies. There was also a television in the alcove closest to Berks Street and the library. The television was one of those large console models with a tiny picture tube on top and a speaker below it.

I was in gym class at noon and, after hearing about the assassination attempt, went directly to Mitten Hall. Only a handful of students were standing in front of the television. I stood with the others watching as Walter Cronkite stammered through some of his words. He was talking about an assault in Texas that happened earlier that day—one against the UN ambassador Adlai Stevenson—when he hesitated for only a second. It was a second in which he seemed to be frozen. Then he put his glasses on and read an announcement. President Kennedy was dead. He removed his glasses as though without them, he could make sense of the words he had just spoken. Shocked and shivering, I turned and went outside to catch a bus back to my apartment where, not having a television, my roommate and I spent the remainder of that day and most of the next listening to the news on the radio. That night I was alone in the apartment when the doorbell rang.

The visitor was David, a friend I had met earlier that year, a law student at Princeton University whose ancestors dated back to the *Mayflower*. Still shaken, we talked about the assassination. David came from a long line of Democrats, and I had rung doorbells and handed out pamphlets urging people to vote for Kennedy during the campaign. He was no doubt someone my father would have loved, except of course for the circumstances.

But I was not in love with him, nor was he with me. Since our first meeting, he had seemed only to want to play Henry Higgins to my *Pygmalion*. That night, I wanted reassurance. I also wanted sex. Or at least I wanted to know what all the hullabaloo was about, and as the roly-poly feelings I'd been carrying began to dissipate, I became more aware of my extremities.

I stretched my fingers high above my head where they sought and intertwined with his, then flexed my toes and let them relax beneath his—"Socks! You're wearing socks?" I asked, under the circumstances finding that both incredulous and funny. He laughed and said his feet got cold easily, which only made me laugh more until all those feelings of guilt and anxiety I had been feeling for the last thirty-six hours eased, and I felt contentment now.

The following spring, I met Nathan.

I was sitting in the cafeteria on the ground floor of Mitten Hall when I felt someone's eyes on me. That was when I looked up and saw Nathan for the first time. He was dressed in an ROTC uniform, sitting alone at an adjacent table. The attraction was mutual and instantaneous. We talked for a few minutes until I found myself flirting outrageously. "What's your name?" he asked, finally.

"Me," I answered coquettishly.

"Did you say Mia?"

"No. Just me," I answered. I looked at his nametag, which had the letters M-C-C-L-O-E printed across it. It looked like Greek to me. "What's yours?" I asked as he laughed and told me how to pronounce it. We talked until it was time for me to leave. Nathan walked with me to my class in Curtis Hall and asked me to meet him again in the cafeteria the following day. I agreed.

We began seeing one another every afternoon, our dates consisting of long walks through campus and the surrounding neighborhoods. It was a time when tensions between North Philadelphia residents and the police were mounting and would later erupt into the Philadelphia riots, but Nathan and I strolled through the area unnoticed.

After just a few weeks, I invited Nathan to my apartment for dinner. Unfortunately, I had learned nothing about cooking from my mother. Our meal that night consisted of processed veal, sticky rice, and some canned green beans. Nathan, however, ate everything without complaint.

Afterward we sat on the sofa bed in the living room studying for our respective classes. I loved his quiet reserve and was falling in love with him and with his intellect, which I saw as deep, intense, and unquenchable.

I could tell, however, that Nathan was restless. Although he was going to Temple on a scholarship, he was planning to leave before the semester ended to join the army. Becoming an officer was something he had dreamt about since childhood.

In the spring of 1964, the word Vietnam was barely being whispered although by then three American presidents had been involved in helping the South Vietnamese army battle with the North. In April of that year, while most Americans were not even sure where Vietnam was located, the US government was pouring two million dollars a day into that country in an effort to defeat communism. The word Vietnam was a word that was about to become as explosive as the country itself.

When Nathan left for basic training in April, I thought the relationship was over. But he wrote to me daily, promising to return as soon as possible. He kept his promise in July arriving in the middle of the night on the fourth.

To confirm the pregnancy three months later—it took that long in those days—I made an appointment with a doctor whose office was close to Temple. He confirmed the pregnancy and, although he had never met Nathan and had met me only once, told me I could not possibly hold on to Nathan. Then he added that Nathan would be unfaithful.

I tried to dismiss his words but they stuck with me, making me feel like one of those voodoo dolls I had recently heard about on television. I felt as though pins were stuck in my heart and in my limbs. Later I tried again to dismiss his predictions as an old man's foolishness, but his words haunted me, ringing like the sound of a death knell.

Nathan and I were married in October by a justice of the peace in Ardmore and then again on our first anniversary by a Catholic priest. After a week spent together at Fort Devens in Massachusetts where Nathan was receiving his MOS training, I returned alone to Pennsylvania. From Fort Devens, Nathan was sent to Fort Wolters in Texas where I joined him in January of 1965.

It was a cold day in December, just before Christmas in 2004. I could hear the wind howling outside Dr. A's office. Although a winter storm was being predicted, there were no snowflakes on the ground when I arrived. When Dr. A, dressed in his usual white shirt opened at the collar, came to greet me. I was sitting in the waiting room, engrossed in a book I was reading.

"What are you reading?" he asked once we were seated in his office. I held the book up. It was another of Delbanco's. This one was *What Remains*. "I read it once before," I told him. "I loved it so much I memorized some of his passages. Now I'm reading it again."

What Remains is the story of a German Jewish family's arrival in New York after the Holocaust. I handed the book to Dr. A, and while he examined it, I continued talking, telling him how as a child I had never learned about the Holocaust at St. Raymond's.

"Later, when I mentioned that fact to a childhood friend, she told me we *had* studied the Holocaust in school. 'I must have been absent that day,' I had quipped. Later, however, I remembered seeing pictures of the Holocaust at home."

Dr. A put the book on the table beside me as I told him about the rec room my father had built in the basement of our house after we moved to West Oak Lane.

"There was a laundry room behind it," I said, "with an old wringer washer that stood between the stationary tub and the cabinet my father built. The cabinet was for canned goods, which were supposed to stave off starvation in the event of a nuclear war with Russia. On top of the cabinet were magazines stacked almost to the ceiling.

"There were *National Geographic* magazines there with pictures of naked women along with copies of *Saturday Evening Post* and *Time*. In one of the *Time* magazines, I found more pictures of naked people, but these were pictures of dead people who had been tossed one on top of another after death. Their bodies were skeletal. "And," I said as I shivered, "they were piled higher than the coal was piled in Pittston."

"So, in retrospect, you had heard of the Holocaust."

"Yes, but I had never heard the word 'holocaust' used in connection with it until I got to Temple. After hearing about it, I started reading every book I could find on the Holocaust. When I finished with nonfiction, I started reading fiction. I was reading a book on the Holocaust in 1965 when I joined Nathan in Texas. When I got there, it was cold outside the way it is today. It was colder than I had realized it could be in Texas.

"About a week after I arrived, I was lying in bed next to Nathan, reading a novel. The novel's antagonist was a particularly gruesome Nazi colonel."

I got up from the sofa then and walked to the window, looking out as though looking for something far away. "When I met Nathan," I began, and then I faltered and stopped. "When I met Nathan"—I tried again—"there was something about him. I can't say that Nathan was sweet. Nathan would never have stood for that. But there was something…Nathan was so young when we got married. He was only nineteen. Too young even to get a marriage license from city hall, and his mother had to go with us.

"I once took a snapshot of Nathan while he slept on the living room floor in the house we were renting in Texas. In the picture, he exuded innocence." I turned from the window then and returned to the sofa. "Anyway, Nathan loved the army, and he was proud of the uniforms he wore.

"One night several weeks after I arrived, Nathan gathered all his fatigues into a bundle and stuffed them into his dress uniform to take to the cleaners in the morning. He sat the bundle on the chair in front of the vanity table and turned it toward the mirror. Then, to be funny, he put his dress pants beneath it and topped it off with his hat.

"Within minutes of getting into bed, Nathan was asleep. As I continued reading about the colonel, I became increasingly aware of the laundry, sitting on the opposite side of the room. Deep into the night, the laundry took on the sinister appearance of the Nazi colonel in the book I was reading. The image became sharper and sharper until I could no longer stand to look at it. Exhausted, I turned out the light, but the bundle looked even more sinister in the moonlit room." Dr. A, who had put his fingers together to form a steeple, moved his hands away from his face and watched me intently.

"Finally, I got up and went into the living room to sleep on the sofa, which is where Nathan found me when he got up for work at five in the morning.

"'What's wrong?' he asked. 'Why are you sleeping here?' When I told him I hadn't slept because his laundry kept reminding me of the Nazi soldier I was reading about, Nathan held me until I fell asleep. The colonel disappeared that day, and I never saw him again.

"Our son was born two weeks later," I said as I took a deep breath. "After that, the army began demanding more and more of Nathan's time. The army was gearing up, getting the soldiers ready for Vietnam. Nathan was spending so much time away from me, I began thinking about what that doctor in North Philadelphia said and as time passed, I became obsessed with his words."

Dr. A looked as though he were about to say something, but I interrupted. "It's like what Dr. Phil says, or is it Chopra? I can't remember which. Anyway, one of them says, 'What you think, you create.'"

Dr. A, who had never seen Dr. Phil on television, said nothing.

"Then one night, it was late, and I was alone in the house in Texas. I was standing in the doorway between the kitchen and the dining room while Nathan was out on maneuvers. I remember standing there that night, wondering where the script was."

"The script?" Dr. A asked.

"Yes," I said. "I felt so ill at ease in my marriage, so unprepared for marriage I found myself looking for a script."

"Before that, who gave you a script?"

I thought for a moment before I answered. "My mother," I said.

"What else do you remember about those days?"

"When I first met Nathan, I loved his quiet reserve. In Texas, however, it did not feel like quiet reserve. It felt as though there was a wall between us and I couldn't figure out how to get around it."

Dr. A leaned forward. "Was it a wall?" he asked. "Or was it a chasm?"

I thought for a moment before I answered. Then I took a deep breath. "It was a chasm."

Our second child, Cynthia, was born just before Nathan left for Officers' Candidate School. I was eight months pregnant with Jessica when Nathan got orders for Vietnam. However, problems on the West Coast delayed his departure, and he was able to return for her birth.

From her earliest moments, Jessi—with her head full of curly black hair and her dark, almost black eyes that locked into mine whenever I fed her—had a personality different from her siblings. Even at one, her older sister, Cynthia, was graceful and feminine, intelligent, and too shy to disturb the status quo. Eric, who at two was built like a quarterback, moved through life with a twinkle in his eyes and a determination to conquer everything he encountered. Both Eric and Cindi were quiet and gentle, while Jessi was forceful and gregarious. She was always ready to talk, even to strangers. In Jessi's world, there were no strangers.

The night before Nathan left for Vietnam, I discovered he was having an affair.

I started telling Dr. A something else when he stopped me. "Wait," he said, "You can't make a statement like that and just go on. How did it happen? How did you learn about the affair?"

I closed my eyes and for a long time I said nothing. Then I opened them and looked at him. "We were back up North by then, living in Philadelphia. That night I walked into the kitchen while Nathan was talking on the phone.

"'Who are you talking to?' I asked from the doorway and he answered saying, 'My girlfriend.' It was a joke, something he had said before, something he meant to be funny, but was not. Somehow, this time, I knew it was not a joke. This time I knew it was true." I was quiet now, concentrating on the pattern on the floor beneath my feet.

"What happened then?" Dr. A asked.

I sighed, but continued. "I backed out of the kitchen and leaned against the dining room wall. I was doubled over, holding both hands in front of my stomach. I had just given birth by Caesarian section and my stomach felt as though it needed to be protected."

"And what did you say to Nathan?"

"Nothing. I said nothing. I lay in bed beside him that night feeling as though my world had suddenly turned sideways and said nothing. Instead, I started to question everything. Everything I had ever believed in. I didn't know anymore what was true and what was false. I didn't know what I could trust and what I could not. I even wondered if God existed.

"The next day I watched through a window as Nathan boarded a plane for the west coast."

"And you said nothing to Nathan? You didn't tell him what you were feeling?" he asked. Dr. A was leaning forward in his chair. He was almost close enough to touch me.

"No." I whispered. "I wanted to, but when I opened my mouth to talk, no words came out." I felt the tears behind my eyes, but blinked them away. I was determined not to cry. "I wanted to pummel my fists against Nathan's chest, but when I moved to do it, nothing happened. I felt immobilized–paralyzed."

Dr. A sat back. "Do you realize," he said, "that you used almost those exact words before?"

"When?" I asked, blinking and not remembering.

"The first time you came here," he said. You were describing the little boy in your dream. Do you remember?" And suddenly I did.

THE MADNESS OF THE GODS

Sometimes, I would get to therapy and start talking, jumping from one subject to another, feeling as though I were getting nowhere. Then, Dr. A would ask a question or make a comment, and I would hear the *click, click*, clicking sound an abacus makes when things begin to add up.

"I watched the Eagles game yesterday," I told him one Monday morning in November.

"It was a good game."

"Yes, but watching it alone made me feel lonely. Then again, maybe when you watch it with someone else, you can't really share it."

"Yes, you can."

A lot of help he is, I thought.

"Tell me what you liked about it."

"I love watching the connection a quarterback makes when he throws a football to a receiver, especially when the receiver catches it, especially when the receiver is in the end zone."

He smiled.

What am I talking about? I wondered. *Why am I talking about football?* "Dr. A, we spend so much time talking about my mother. I thought, well, we almost never talk about my dad."

"I suspect it's too painful for you."

"You're probably right." I was lost in thought for a moment until I looked up. I was sitting in the chair by the window. It was a chilly, breezy day outside in the quaint, upscale town of Jenkintown where Dr. A's office was located. Jenkintown was a small town where commercialism was frowned upon and where fast food restaurants had long ago been banned. Dr. A's office was warm and comfortable and in sharp contrast to the weather in the town outside his window. I looked from the window and saw Dr. A, waiting for me to continue.

"When I was a little girl, my dad was like one of those football players. He was my hero. But once I came out of the hospital, everything changed. After that, I felt so alone. For the rest of my life whenever I needed someone to talk to, I felt alone."

"What about therapy?"

I smiled, "Even therapists are not as handy as you'd like to think they are."

"So what's been your solution?"

I laughed. "When I need help, I go to the library, or the book-store. When my son was born, Nathan and I were in Texas, and I was disconnected from my family. Neither he nor I had any experience with children.

"He was an only child, and even though I was twelve when my youngest sister was born, I can't remember ever being allowed to hold her. Before Eric was born, I bought a copy of Dr. Spock's book on childcare. I can remember being up nights, holding Eric with my left hand and holding a copy of the book in my right.

"Much later after I met Vincent and was feeling insecure, I went to the library, typed the words 'insecure love' into the com-puter, and found a perfect match. The book I found said inse-cure love has been around for forever. It said the Greeks called it the madness of the gods. I had to laugh at that, but that feeling of insecurity was no joke. I felt as though it had been around me forever."

"After Nathan and I separated, the kids and I lived in a rental property. I bought a car for $250. It was the ugliest car in the world, but I didn't care. It ran just long enough for me to go back to Temple and get my degree. Afterward, I went to work for a weekly newspaper. I was putting the whole thing together by myself. I even delivered it. But I wasn't making enough money to support myself and my children.

"One day, my parents came to visit. They took one look at the rental property falling down around us and asked if I wanted to move back to Pennsylvania. My father put a security deposit on an apartment in Elkins Park. Then he took me to Sears and bought furniture for the new apartment. He even gave me a used car to get around in."

"So your father did rescue you after all."

I laughed, "Yes I suppose he did. But—"

"But what?"

"One day, I was standing outside the apartment with him, and I said 'I love you, Dad,' and he said nothing. Later, I wondered if he'd heard me."

"Was he standing far from you?"

"No, he was standing two feet away, facing me.

"It's no wonder," he said, "that you find beauty in a football game."

LIKE WHAT RUMI SAID
ABOUT LOVERS

It was four years after therapy began, and I was telling Dr. A about the end of my marriage. It didn't end when Nathan came back from Vietnam. Somehow, we managed to stay together.

"When it did end," I told him, "it ended almost to the day that Saigon fell. I went into a coma after that and the world did too, or at least it seemed to. Later, I felt untethered, unable to hold on to anything I reached for. In the twenty-five years between the divorce and the new millennium, I moved nine times and worked almost twice as many jobs. I did everything from waitressing to teaching at a Catholic school.

"I had two long-term relationships. One in New Jersey and another after I moved back to Pennsylvania. But they were mostly superficial." I had been looking at Dr. A as I spoke, but now, I looked down. "Mostly sexual."

Dr. A said nothing as tears came to my eyes. "It was the only way I knew how to be intimate," I whispered. "By the time I met Vincent in 2001, it had been almost eighteen years since I dated." We were both quiet a moment until I continued. "Then after I turned sixty, I went to work for the school district. I started driving a school bus, and I love it."

"What do you love about it?"

"Everything," I told him. "I love being outdoors. I love listening to the sound of children talking. I love the hours, the early mornings, and late afternoons when I can see the sunrise and set. And I love being high up in the driver's seat like the big boys."

He smiled. "And what don't you like about it?"

I thought for a moment before I answered, "Sometimes when I am driving an eighty-four-passenger bus across a bridge where I can look down on another highway, I get dizzy and feel as though I'm falling."

"Sometimes you can feel that way," he explained. "You can feel as though you are falling through the sky, if a situation you are in is falling apart."

I was silent.

"So, what's falling apart?"

"Everything," I told him, ready now to talk about Vincent.

The first time I spoke to him, I asked some inane question I could have asked anyone. I chose Vincent because I knew, as president of our union, he could give me the best answer and because I wanted his attention. That was late in November of 2001.

I had gone to work for the school district back in March, and by the end of May, I had flunked two tests. The first was the driving exam I needed to get my commercial driver's license. All I had to do was take one look at the state trooper, administering the test, and I knew I was in trouble. He looked exactly like every Southern police chief I had ever seen—in real life and in the movies—with a toothpick in one corner of his mouth, one hand on his holster, and the other on the oversized belt buckle underneath his belly.

The other test was a mammogram. The results showed a suspicious spot on my right breast. I needed a biopsy, but because I was in denial (and because after all dear God, I can handle only one crisis at a time), I kept postponing the biopsy until after I received my CDL (commercial driver's license).

Finally, I called to set up the biopsy, which was then scheduled for Friday, the thirteenth. The doctor who administered it was a compassionate young woman who said I was about to feel a tiny prickle on my skin that would not hurt a bit. It hurt like hell and to make matters worse, I had to wait an entire week for the results. I went home and tried not to think about it.

Home at that time was the mother-in-law suite in my youngest daughter's house. Jessi lived upstairs with her husband and four children, while I shared the apartment in the basement with my mother who was eighty-seven and had been living with us for two years.

Because my mother liked to keep the television on all day, I spent most of that week outdoors. It was peaceful, sitting there in the shade of an old maple tree. I spent most of the summer there. In July, the mornings were cool and chilly, reminding me of the spring morning—several years earlier—that I spent in Darmstadt, Germany, with my son and his wife as we waited outside the local mall, the Luisen Platz, for a bus to take me to the airport and back home again.

In August, the temperatures rose to over one hundred degrees. It was the first free summer I had had since childhood, and I found it idyllic. Both my mother's close proximity and my concerns about the test results stirred memories long forgotten. While I waited for the results, I began writing about my childhood. I was under the shade of that tree when my cell phone rang. When I got the results, I cried with relief. Then, I picked my pen up and continued writing.

My mom stayed with my sister Joanne that Labor Day weekend, and the apartment was unusually quiet. I celebrated my birthday that weekend, and as the humidity lessened and the temperatures dropped, I turned off the air conditioner and allowed the first autumn breezes to blow through the apartment.

At some point on Friday, I noticed the television was on, but the sound was down. I leaned in to turn it off, but something stopped me. I was afraid I might miss something, some important announcement that would keep me connected to the rest of the world.

I returned to work the day after Labor Day, happy to be back. The building we worked in was a one-story, red brick garage located behind the high school, which was itself red brick and rustic, looking like something straight out of *Happy Days*.

There was a lounge in the bus garage where the drivers spent their down time. During the previous school year, I had noticed how well everyone got along there. I could walk into that lounge, see a dozen different people, and realize there was only one conversation happening and everyone was included.

About a week after school started, I walked into the lounge just before nine. One driver was back from his run. His name was Tom, and his eyes were glued to the television.

"Look," he said when he saw me. "An airplane just crashed into a building in New York City." I looked at the screen and saw flames shooting from the side of an office building. Believing a small plane had slammed into the building, and the fire would be contained quickly, I clocked out and went home.

When I got there, my mom had the television on. I turned to the television and felt stunned and horrified as yet another plane hit the second tower. An hour later, I was talking to my son, who still lived in Germany, when I saw the first tower collapse. There must be a video delay because when I screamed, he was not seeing what I was seeing. I continued watching, incredulous as news of the strike on the Pentagon, whose very name meant strength and invulnerability, was struck and as innocent people fell to their deaths. I was horrified by the fact that thousands of people died that day, not at war, but at work; not behind guns and bullets, but behind desks and reams of paper.

My brain seemed to buckle under the weight of that day. Nineteen hours later, I was still trying to process the enormity of the event. That night, I dreamt I was moving back and forth from one tower to the other, trying to keep each erect, but I could not. During the day, I was constantly sitting in front of the television. I wanted my life back the way it was before the attack. I wanted to return to a life without terror. I wanted to look at the sky and not be afraid.

I continued watching television until finally I realized I was looking for that one story that would reassure me—that one story that would put everything back the way it was. I got up then and put a moratorium on watching television, knowing that without at least one moment of complete and absolute silence, I would never be able to move forward.

Finally, there came a morning when I looked up at the sky, saw a helicopter moving safely through it and thanked God for the miracle of flight. When *Time* magazine announced Mayor Giuliani as their Man of the Year, I found myself thinking, *You see, Santa there really is a Rudolph.* I knew my sense of humor, however oblique, was returning.

Things were different, however. I was different. The feelings that stirred inside me after 9/11 made me feel like part of a community, and for once, I did not feel alone. Later, I wondered if all the feelings 9/11 stirred inside me led me to feel the way I did about Vincent.

When I asked him my inane question that day, he was standing about three feet away from me. As he answered, he started walking toward me, so close in fact that by the time he finished, he was standing inside my personal space. At which point, he stopped and smiled.

———— ✆ ————

"When you went to work at the school district, were you looking for someone like Vincent?" Dr. A asked.

"No. I wasn't looking for anyone. But maybe I was hoping. I just never expected to find anyone. Vincent came as such a surprise to me. Later, he said to me, 'I thought all those days were behind me, until you came along.'"

"If you had been looking, what do you think you would have been looking for?"

"Someone sweet, I think. Yes. Definitely sweet, and Vincent was that. Dr. A, after Nathan, I never even put those two words together in the same sentence."

"Which two words?"

"Sweet and man. I never even thought a man could be sweet."

"It was an oxymoron?"

"Yes, and when I met Vincent, he was that—exactly." I had been looking down as I spoke, but now, I looked at the doctor. "Dr. A, I never really felt as though I met Vincent. It's more like what Rumi said about lovers—that they don't meet, but that 'they are in one another all along.' It was as though when I saw him, I recognized him."

IN PAPER CUPS
INSTEAD OF CHINA

Vincent and I had downtime together every morning when we both went back to the garage to report to our dispatcher, Jim. I always got there after Vincent and stood in the doorway, listening as the two men talked, their conversation occasionally drowned out by the screams of emergency vehicles, racing in constant pursuit of threats caused by fears of anthrax infestations.

Two days before Thanksgiving, my bus, an old dilapidated thing on loan from another school district, lost its transmission in the middle of my early morning run. Jim called a tow truck for the bus and sent Vincent to rescue me. We delivered the student safely to a school in a neighboring district and, on the drive back, had a few minutes alone during which he told me he was a widower, that his wife had died of breast cancer five years earlier and that they had been married for almost forty years.

A few days after my bus broke down, I was on my way to the lounge for a staff meeting I was already late for when I noticed Vincent sitting in his car. As I approached, he rolled down the window. "Aren't you going to the meeting?" I asked.

"No," he answered.

Of course, I wanted to see more of him so I said, "If you don't go, you'll get written up."

He just laughed at that. He came inside, however. Before the meeting, chairs were set up in rows across the room with additional chairs lining both walls. When Vincent came in, he sat across from me. During the meeting, I looked at him and saw that his eyes were closed. I stole that moment to study his face, which looked so much like Regis Philbin's. I continued looking at his face, memorizing every detail until I realized I could see his face with my eyes closed. Later I realized I could see it even with my eyes open.

If I could draw, I could show you exactly what he looked like at that moment with his full head of hair that was more salt than pepper and combed back, Fonzarelli style, with a single curl falling to the middle of his forehead. Later, I would realize his best trait was the way he stood with his head tilted in my direction while I talked to him about almost anything.

Dr. A was silent a moment. "Do you realize," he said, "that in your first two encounters with Vincent he fulfilled all your requirements?"

"What do you mean?"

"The first time, when you asked what you called your inane question, he walked right past that chasm, never even knowing it was there. And later, not only did he open that window, he came right through it."

I laughed when he said that.

From the very beginning—and to this day—I felt a pull toward Vincent, like a magnetic force. By early December, I was seeing Vincent everywhere—at the time clock, in the yard, and even on the road.

His best friend was a man named Luke, who was quickly becoming my friend too. He used to join Vincent on his bus early every morning, and the two of them would sit and talk before their runs. One day, Luke invited me along. During the next few months, Vincent and I became friends. After awhile, Luke stopped coming in early, and it was just Vincent and me.

I used to love those early morning talks. I had never had a relationship like it. It reminded me of growing up in West Oak Lane where every morning I would wake up to the sound of my parents' voices as they sat talking to one another at the dining room table. From my bedroom, which was directly above them, I could smell the coffee, percolating and hear the tintinnabulation of the china cups as they were set on top of their saucers.

Now, with Vincent, I had someone to talk to about the little things—the things that make up a day and a lifetime, and I started bringing coffee with me every morning—in paper cups instead of china. I was falling in love, and as scary as that was for me, it was also exquisite.

I was, however, becoming impatient waiting for Vincent to take the relationship to another level. I was dreaming about him at night, and in my dreams, he was so real, so present, that sometimes I would wake up sure he was right there beside me. He appeared in my dreams so often I began to feel as though there was some part of him that existed apart from space and time. I don't know any other way to express it.

Time passed, and I began to wonder if he noticed I was attracted to him. He did not seem to know, although God knows everyone else at the garage noticed. But I didn't care. I went to work and came home. I spent time with my children and grandchildren. I was happier than I had ever been before. For me time, structured time, seemed to have lifted itself away and all the events in my life flowed gently, one into another. I had lost all sense of calendar or clock time and had it not been so obvious,

I would hardly have noticed that the Christmas holidays were quickly approaching.

The day after our Christmas party, I saw Vincent in the lounge talking to another driver, a friend of his and a fellow union officer named Jack. Vincent was eating a slice of leftover pie right out of the tin plate it came in.

"Did you eat the whole pie?' I asked, interrupting their conversation.

Jack had been talking to Vincent but now he froze in mid-sentence. He looked at Vincent, and Vincent looked back at him. Jack smiled at Vincent, and my face reddened. Inside my head, I imagined Jack's look said, *She's really crazy about you*, and Vincent's said, *I know*. In actuality, however, Jack's look probably said, *She's really crazy*, and Vincent's said, *I know*.

One evening, Jessi and I went to see the movie *A Beautiful Mind*. Afterward, I realized I was feeling exactly the way Nash had. I was beginning to question whether Vincent actually existed or if he was a product of my imagination. Oh, I knew he existed—out there. But did he exist "out there" in relation to me? Or were all our interactions a product of my desires? All that changed however the night he called to ask me to go out with him.

WHAT I ALWAYS WANTED

Vincent called to invite me to dinner with him and Luke. It had been a very long time since I'd been out on a date, and I was under the impression I was supposed to play hard-to-get, so I turned him down.

"Really?" Jessi said when I told her. "Mom, the fifties are over. Call him back and tell him yes."

"Really?" I asked her.

"Yes, Mom. Call him back and tell him you changed your mind. Tell him you were having a senior moment. Tell him anything, just call him back."

I called him back and told him I would love to have dinner with him—and Luke. On Saturday morning, I asked Jessi to go to the mall with me, so I could buy something new to wear. I was so excited that at the entrance to the mall, I literally walked into a glass wall I thought was a partially opened door, but was not.

When it happened, Jessi and I started laughing and crying simultaneously.

"Mom," she said, "you slammed into that wall so hard, you bounced right off it." Despite the laughter, I had injured my face and my right eye started swelling up immediately.

"Everyone at work knows I'm going out with Vincent this weekend," I told Jessi, who, at that time, was also a driver. It was virtually impossible to keep anything secret for long at the bus garage. With less than forty drivers, anything out of the ordinary was noticed immediately. Once, while I was sitting on the sofa in the lounge, Vincent sat down beside me. A hush fell over the room as Vincent, speaking softly, asked if I liked the haircut he had just gotten. I looked at his full head of hair and smiled.

"On the sofa?" my daughter asked incredulously. "In front of everybody?" After that, people started talking, wondering about the relationship between us.

"When I walk into work on Monday, I'm going to have a black eye." At that, we both started laughing again.

The evening went so well, Vincent asked me to go to dinner with him (and Luke) again on Sunday. All three of us went out for three or four consecutive weekends and at the end of each evening, Vincent took me home and kissed me good night.

It did not matter to me that Luke went with us. Vincent could have brought a whole football stadium full of people along. (Once, he almost did. It was Vincent and me and at least a dozen of his closest friends—all of whom he wanted me to meet.) I didn't care. All I cared about was being with Vincent.

I had always had trouble relating to people one-on-one, and the day we had our first date together—without Luke—was no exception. The night before, I kept waking up to see if it was morning yet. I spent the entire day feeling a mixture of excitement and dread as I waited for Vincent to arrive. But when I saw him, all my anxieties dissipated. Later, when he took me home, he told me he enjoyed it, "every minute of it." I was ecstatic.

One day while Vincent and I were talking together outside the garage, one of the drivers walked past. "Watch out for him," she said, "he's dangerous." I laughed at that, laughed at the thought of Vincent as dangerous and laughed with delight at being recognized as among the people having a relationship.

Knowing my propensity for fast-food, Vincent seemed delighted to take me to country inns and fine restaurants, and I delighted in sitting across the table from him. Once after telling Vincent I was ordering veal, I listened to the specials and changed my mind.

"I'll have the seafood," I told the waitress.

Vincent looked at me. "Order what you want," he said.

I smiled and, looking directly at him, said, "I already have what I want." *What I always wanted*, I thought to myself. Vincent just kind of rolled his eyes and went back to looking at the menu.

"Will we always be friends?" I asked one night after thinking about my ex-husband who had one day walked away and never looked back. Vincent answered, "Always."

We were watching the news together on another night when a story came on about three people who had died in the Middle East that weekend. Earlier, we had seen a story on the local news about three people who had been murdered in South Philadelphia that same weekend. When I told Vincent, "Americans aren't safe anywhere," he turned to me and said, "You're safe here."

Unable to express my feelings verbally, I found a card that was blank inside and wrote "All I want for Christmas I got the day I met you," and gave it to him during our first Christmas together. He loved it.

"Look at her," Jim said to our transportation director, Mike, one day when the three of us were standing in the lounge together one afternoon. "She's glowing. She looks just like Mary Tyler Moore did just before she threw her hat in the air."

Halfway through our second year together, however Vincent was backing away from me. His behavior made me feel as though I were walking along a road that suddenly disappeared. I felt as though I were staring sightless into the thick fog of a thousand tomorrows. At first, I denied my feelings. Feeling disconnected from Vincent, I became disconnected from myself too.

During some weekends, we would have plans, while during others, he was noticeably absent. Sometimes even when he was right beside me, he would seem far away. But at other times, we would wake up together, and he would reach for me. The circumstances changed one way and then back again so quickly my head felt as though it were spinning in circles the way Regan's did in *The Exorcist*. I was more insecure than ever, certain it was something I had done.

One weekend when feelings of abandonment threatened to take over my psyche, I felt compelled to jump into my car and drive to New Jersey. It didn't matter that it was the middle of winter. It didn't matter that it was five in the morning. I told myself if I stopped for breakfast on the way, it would be after seven and the sun would be up by the time I got there.

I arrived in Ocean City just after seven. I knew this city well having come to it with my family since I was a small girl. Nothing had changed during those years except the size of the rental properties. I loved it here, and I had even spent a summer here back when I was in college. Traveling to Ocean City was like visiting an old friend who lived far away.

I parked my car as close to the ocean as possible, then climbed the steps to the boardwalk. The sight of the ocean thrilled me. Despite the cold and the wind, I stood there entranced for more than an hour. I listened to the roar of the waves as they tumbled toward the shore. I tried to memorize the way they looked and the way they sounded, so I could take them away with me when I left.

I needed this ocean. I needed its immensity and its immediacy. Its size put my problems into perspective, making them seem insignificant. When I was ready, I got back into my car and drove home.

"It's not you, it's me," Vincent told me once, but of course, I did not believe him. I knew it was me. It had to be me. Besides, if it were me, I could fix it. (Even if it were him, I could change it, I told myself, all the while knowing that change only comes from within.)

It was about a week later after my car had been struck by another driver and was in a body shop that I asked Vincent to drive me home. When we got to my door, I said, "You drove me to the wrong home." He smiled but seemed distracted and distant. I missed him even before I got out of the car.

The next morning, I felt so wounded I couldn't get out of bed. I just lay there, thinking about all the things I was missing. I missed Vincent, and I missed my car. I missed Jessi, who was working nights at a local television station and slept all day. I missed my son who lived in another country and my daughter Cindi who lived in another county. I also missed my mother who had just gone to live with my sister, Joanne.

During the next school year, Vincent and I continued spending every morning together. Once summer arrived, however, I saw him only twice. It was the loneliest summer of my life, one in which I was sure I was losing my mind. In September, I reached for the phone and found Dr. A.

"Dr. A," I asked one day during our fourth year of therapy, "why do relationships end? Why do people wind up with broken hearts?" The question of course was rhetorical, and I went on to other topics, other questions. I talked for another forty minutes. At the end of the session, Dr. A asked a question.

"How are things going with Cindi?" After my youngest daughter remarried, I moved in with my daughter Cindi, who had recently separated from her husband. At first, I had not been able to decide whether or not to move. Then I talked to my friend Jim at work and told him about my dilemma. "Go where you are most needed," he said, and I did.

"When I first moved in," I told Dr. A, "I wanted to do everything. I wanted to help with everything, but after a few weeks, I realized I couldn't, and I became more careful about the things I volunteered to do. I didn't want to make promises I could not keep."

"That's your answer," Dr. A said with a smile.

"My answer to what?" I asked.

"To the question you asked earlier. Why do relationships end? They end because in the beginning, people make more promises than they are able to keep," he said.

"When does it end?" I asked Dr. A several weeks later. "When will therapy be over for me?" I was not really expecting an answer, but Dr. A answered immediately.

"When it all becomes conscious," he said. "When you find your trigger and start making the connection."

"When all of what becomes conscious?" I asked, not sure what he was talking about.

Dr. A smiled. "Let's go back a little bit," he said as I pulled myself up a little straighter although inwardly I was groaning. "How did you feel when you discovered Nathan was unfaithful?"

"Sad. Hurt. Upset. Abandoned. Alone. All of the above and more."

"And how did you feel when Vincent started moving away from you?"

"The same."

"Okay," he said, "and what happens to you when you feel that way?" I just looked at him, not understanding his question.

"Think about it," he said." Where were you the first time you felt that way?"

"In the hospital," I said, not needing to think about it.

"And what happens when you feel that way? What happened the first time you felt abandoned?"

"I felt paralyzed, unable to move or even to talk." "Exactly," he said. "Do you remember telling me that when you returned from the hospital, your sister was surprised that you remembered how to walk?" I nodded. "You didn't forget how to walk. You forgot how to *talk*. You forgot how to interact with other people. And I suspect," he said, "that you feel that way more often than you're telling me and when that happens—"

"That's the trigger," I said, understanding it now. "Whenever I feel rejected, I go back inside that hospital. At least, inside my own mind."

"Yes," Dr. A said, "you go back inside that hospital. You withdraw, and you wait for someone to rescue you."

"But no one ever does."

"No," Dr. A agreed. "But when it all becomes conscious, when you realize after it happens that you have sent yourself back into that hospital, then you can go in there and rescue yourself." Dr. A went on talking, explaining that he thought I had sent myself back into that hospital sometimes for weeks and even for months.

I sat forward almost on the edge of the chair, trying to grasp the full import of his words. *Was he right?* I wondered. *Had I really spent that much time back inside that hospital?* I remembered the months I had spent "in a coma" after Nathan left and the deep loneliness I felt during the summer of 2003. I looked up to tell Dr. A how I felt, but he was way ahead of me.

"When you can see it right after you put yourself there, when you see it and can take yourself out again immediately, you will have found the trigger that propels your behavior."

But it would take another couple of years before I could see how fast and how often I put myself into that hospital. And it would take another therapist before I could see that trigger in action. When that happened, I could then go inside that hospital and rescue myself almost immediately.

RUDE
AWAKENING

Love takes off masks that we fear we cannot live without and know we cannot live within.

—James Baldwin

IN SOLITUDE AND IN SILENCE

At our next meeting, Dr. A and I talked about the convent. In high school, as I continued to feel distant from other people, I started going to daily mass. I had always loved the mysterious and exotic sounds of the Latin Mass. I found beauty in the ritual and comfort in its repetition.

When the bells rang three times at the start of the Consecration, the vibrations between each brought me to a sweet, sacred silence, in which I felt as though I existed inside the mind of God. Just before graduation, I became convinced I should enter a convent. At the time, it seemed like a good idea.

As summer ended and the day I was to leave arrived, it became increasingly important to me to spend my last hours at home under the awning over the front patio. That, however, turned out to be impossible because that was the day hurricane Donna, which had slammed into the Florida Keys and blown its way north, slipped into Philadelphia in the middle of the night. The weather forecasters were calling it "the tail end of a hurricane," but it felt full force to me as the wind howled all night and the skies let loose with a rainfall whose force I had never seen before.

In the morning, I awoke to the sound of raindrops, pounding themselves against the windowpanes of my room. As I dressed, things seemed to be happening slowly. It was almost as though they were happening in slow motion and under water.

I donned the black dress and regulation undergarments that were to become my uniform, then joined my parents in the dining room. Later as the three of us rode toward Chestnut Hill, we sat in silence. When we arrived, my father dropped my mother and me off at the door while he parked the car. My mother and I ran toward the entrance, but a gust of wind forced the rain against our backs, and we were soaked through before making it inside. (Back at home, as I later learned, the wind had just ripped the green canvas awning in two.)

Finally, the moment arrived. I had entered the convent.

More than one hundred girls entered the convent with me that day, and although a new building had been built to accommodate all of us, it wasn't quite complete when we arrived. There was also a delay in the arrival of our textbooks and classes were postponed indefinitely. As a result, we were left with a surprising amount of unstructured time.

If I had entered the convent hoping for intimacy and solitude, our numbers alone made that impossible. Just as in high school, I was desperate to make connections with others but found it impossible to initiate conversations. My sense of isolation heightened.

There were no radios, no telephones, and no clocks in the convent, and I felt trapped inside. Never knowing the time made reality feel gossamer.

We slept in one large room on the second floor of the new building that was partitioned into tiny cells, one for each of us. At night, I would lay there, listening as too many of the other girls, all of them homesick, cried themselves to sleep. Most of the girls tried to muffle the sounds by crying into their pillows, but it didn't help much.

I never cried. Instead, I lay there, still and silent as my mind raced in every direction until finally I was convinced there was some trick to falling asleep that I had forgotten.

One night, I heard the sound of a church bell as it tolled two, three, and finally four times before I fell asleep. On another night, the ordinary sound of a car passing was enough to comfort me, and I felt less alone.

Looking back later, I marveled that I ever left the convent because despite the loneliness, it was exactly what I had imagined it would be. Later, I remembered the stillness and serenity of those days, days that moved quietly and gently one after the other. Despite all of that, however, I was aware that something was missing there.

Then one night, I stayed awake, trying to imagine what the future would hold for me if I left the convent. Somehow, I knew there was something out there waiting for me, and I decided to leave.

Once back at home, I found a job, working for an insurance company directly across the street from the Philadelphia Museum of Art. It was late October, and the leaves on the trees had already begun changing their colors. I took the subway to city hall every morning and walked along the Benjamin Franklin Parkway past some of the most beautiful buildings in the world. The crunch of the leaves beneath my feet and the sweetness of the outdoor air were exhilarating, especially after the confines of the convent.

"When you were talking about the convent," Dr. A said, "you said something was missing. What was it?"

"It was God. God was missing. When I entered the convent, it was with fear and trepidation as though I were about to encounter him around any corner. Once there, however, he eluded me, even in chapel."

"Is he still missing?"

"Yes, but I've been looking for him."

He smiled. "Where have you been looking?"

Now it was my turn to smile. "Mostly in books," I answered. "Dr. A, do you think you can read your way to enlightenment?"

"How can it hurt?"

"Sometimes, I think that for me the path to nirvana lies in the questions," I said, and Dr. A nodded.

Four years after beginning therapy, I was packing to go to the Outer Banks with my daughter Cindi and her family. Just before leaving, I received a letter from the Archdiocese where Nathan was living. I knew he and his third wife were planning to have their marriage blessed in the Church. Jessi had told me her father was seeking an annulment, but I hadn't realized I would be contacted.

As I read the letter, mailed to me in my maiden name, I wondered how many times this man had to divorce me before he considered it final. I put the letter aside and went on vacation.

When I returned another letter was waiting. "The basis for (Nathan's) request," it said, "is the claim that some essential element of the marriage contract did not meet the requirements in Canon Law for validity."

What element? I wondered. Compassion? Concern? Caring? Companionship? The letter mentioned church, canon, civil, contract, Caruso. What were these people talking about? Composure? Consent? Closure? Compassion? I had come full circle. But, somehow, I was back where I began. I grabbed the letter and headed for my appointment with Dr. A.

Just before I left on vacation, I had been driving back to my apartment one day when, at a red light, I watched a man walking across the street. As he walked diagonally away from me, I noticed how much he looked like Nathan when I first met him. His hair looked like Nathan's with its slight Fro, and his walk was Nathan's exactly. I waited to see the man's face, but he never turned around.

As I watched him move, I remembered the way Nathan moved. I had always thought Nathan's movements to be self-assured, but while watching this man imitate Nathan, I saw something I had never thought about before. It was a vulnerability I had taken for granted, or perhaps had totally overlooked in Nathan. Now I had no doubt that this vulnerability was one of the qualities that had attracted me in the first place.

During my meetings with Dr. A, I spoke of my marriage only sporadically, never delving too deeply into the murky waters of those disappointing years. Now I wanted to tell him everything, but as I drove to his office that morning, I wondered if I could rip off all the bandages I had been wearing for so long and expose the wounds underneath.

"While Nathan and I were married," I told Dr. A, "he had a habit that used to drive me crazy. It was something he said, and I suppose, he would say it whenever I was doing something he disliked. He would tell me I was in for a 'rude awakening.' Later, I realized just how prophetic those words turned out to be.

"After he left for Vietnam, the army kept us separated for most of the next five years. Finally, the army sent him to Fort Dix in New Jersey. The kids and I went with him. But the marriage never improved. In desperation, I went to the army's mental health clinic for help.

"During the first session, the psychiatrist suggested marriage counseling and asked me to bring Nathan to the next meeting. I didn't think Nathan would come, but he surprised me by agreeing to meet me there. The doctor met with Nathan and me the first week and then suggested we include the other woman. (At the time, I was not aware that she worked at the mental health clinic.) Reluctantly, I agreed. Later, her fiancé also joined us and a second professional, a psychologist, helped lead the group.

"I'm not sure why, maybe because I felt we were going nowhere, but suddenly one day, I turned to Nathan and, much to the doctor's amazement, asked if he were having an affair. Of course, we all knew he was having an affair, but I wanted to hear it from him. He had always denied it to me in the past, and I wanted to believe him. Before the doctor could stop him, Nathan looked at me and answered, 'Yes.'

"I don't know how to describe my feelings at that moment except to tell you what happened next. With my worst fear confirmed, there was no place for me to hide. No place, but one.

"From that moment on, I remained in therapy for an entire week—at least in my own mind. There was no escape. Inside my mind, I pretended I was asking the doctor a question which, when answered, led to another question and another and another.

"With every answer, I felt as though I were ascending a spiral staircase. I kept this up for the entire week until I reached the ultimate question and received the ultimate answer, an answer that came with an explosion. It was as though I had reached the top of the spiral—the top of the universe. I felt myself burst through that limit until suddenly I was floating on a cloud. But more, much more, for it felt as though the cloud, the universe, and I were all made up of the same substance. I was completely and totally at peace. Actually, 'peace' is too small a word to tell you all I felt in that moment. And yet, it wasn't what I felt; it wasn't what was *there* in that moment but what was *not* there that made that moment so remarkable. There was no worry, no pain, no doubt, and no negative thought. Actually, there were no thoughts at all.

"For that instant, I believed (and I still do) that I did indeed have all the answers to all of the questions. It was as if the entire universe had opened up to show me all its secrets.

"Then that moment ended and was followed by another moment, a moment which was the complete opposite of the first.

Suddenly I felt as though the entire inside of my mind was made up of glass that was shattering into a million tiny pieces. My mind was in complete chaos. There was no order, no structure, and no limit to the madness. I felt as though I had descended into hell, and as soon as I felt the totality of that moment, I was immediately propelled—catapulted—into a third one in which I felt finally, as though I were back on earth, back in reality, except that I could no longer hold on to that reality. Instead, my mind kept bouncing back and forth between the first two moments. It was as though my mind existed at both ends of a seesaw simultaneously. Somehow I knew I had to fight my way—claw my way—back to the middle in order to unite those two very opposite parts of my being.

"It took a long time, but eventually, I was able to control my mind and maintain some kind of balance. For weeks afterward, I felt blessed, like one of the saints pictured in the stained glass windows at St. Raymond's. Or perhaps what I felt was simply relief that I had somehow managed to escape insanity."

"Dr. A," I said the next time we met, "one of the things I learned that day is that there is no such thing as linear time and that all things happen simultaneously. I suppose that another way of saying it is that we don't exist in time, but rather, we exist, and time is superimposed onto us to give us a sense of structure and order, much the same way the lines of latitude and longitude are placed onto a map to give us a sense of place.

"The secrets of the universe aren't really secrets. We all know them all the time. We simply don't know how to access them. Which is why I felt the way I did when I was little, as though I had to pass my grandmother's door on tiptoe. I was afraid to look into her room and see her suffering."

"Are you telling me you believe she is still there? Still suffering?"

"No, Dr. A, there is no still. There is only now. My grandmother's death is happening now—but in a different dimension of time—or in some other universe. I don't know. I don't have the words to explain it. Whatever knowledge I gained that day came to me cognitively without words.

"When I 'came back' from wherever it was I had gone that day, I kept thinking about my grandmother's death, and although it happened ten years before I was born, it was the most important event in my life because it impacted my mother, and in turn, it impacted me."

"When you had that experience, were you reading any of the books on spirituality that you're reading now?"

"No. That experience happened in 1972, and most of those books had yet to be written. At the time, I had no idea what had happened to me. I didn't know how to label it. Without a label, it frightened me. It threatened me, and I never forgot it.

"Then one day, I was reading Raymond Moody's book about near-death experiences, and I realized how similar my experience was to that described by the people having NDEs. Except that I wasn't near death."

"And how do you see that experience now?"

"For months after that, I walked around at the edge of blissfulness. But I didn't know how to maintain it. In those days, there was no *Oprah*. I had never heard of meditation, and in time, those feelings diminished.

"It wasn't until almost fifteen years later that I discovered meditation and not until years after that that I started reading the *Bhagavad Gita*. One line in the *Gita* made me keep coming back to it. The line 'that all of creation is the transformation of the absolute into the relative' resonated with something deep inside me.

"After that experience, I was no longer afraid of dying. Instead—."

"What? What are you afraid of?"

"Sometimes, when I've been alone too long, I'm afraid the madness will come back. Sometimes, I'm even afraid of enlightenment, afraid that if it comes around again, it will hit me again the way it hit me then."

"As a rude awakening?"

"Yes, exactly."

Then one day, I told Dr. A about a book I was reading by a woman named Karen Armstrong, who had once been a nun in an English convent. In it, she said she had trouble with what she called her deep solitude. After she left the convent, she felt like a complete failure until she began studying comparative theology and started writing books on subjects, such as God and the Buddha.

As a writer, she spent most of her days in solitude and in silence. As she wrote, the silence began to vibrate and resonate until she experienced it with an ecstasy and transcendence she never felt as a nun.

Reading that reminded me of something that happened a long time ago. It must have been in about 1999, when I was meditating a lot and listening to Gregorian chant.

I was also reading a book about chant in which the author said chant had originated in medieval times when a group of monks meditated. So deep was their concentration that in their intensity they began to vibrate and, as the vibrations deepened, they suddenly erupted into sound and chant was born.

I closed my eyes and imagined myself vibrating with the universe, vibrating until I, too, began to hum. And I imagined God as he was before he created the universe. I saw him so content with himself that he began to hum, and I saw that humming growing so large it became one great big bang—one huge burst of energy. "Dr. A, do you think it could have happened that way? Do you think it could have been that simple?"

That summer, after I told Dr. A about the therapy at Fort Dix, I went to work at a summer camp. One of the women at the camp was from India, and she invited me to join her at a festival at a Buddhist Temple not far from my apartment.

She introduced me to her husband who seemed to be an especially devout Hindu. As we sat together in the temple talking, he said, "The knowledge we carry inside ourselves is a direct link to the infinite. Enlightenment," he said, "comes when we are ready for it, and we are ready for it when we ask for it."

THE ROSETTA STONE

In 2002, my mother went to live with my sister Joanne and then into a nursing home. I had trouble visiting her there. I hated seeing her locked inside. Sometimes while visiting, I would take her outside to sit in the sunshine. One day, she kept falling asleep, sitting in her wheelchair. At one point, she awoke with a start then looked around to get her bearings.

"I keep nodding off," she said.

"It's okay. I do too," I told her, and she laughed.

Then one day, when she seemed more coherent than usual, she put her hand on my arm and told me one last secret. She said that she was the one who had given her mother the pills that caused the miscarriage.

"What?" I asked as she took her hand away from my arm. "What?" I repeated as I noticed her attention was gone, and it was too late to question her. *What was she telling me?* I wondered, feeling dazed and confused. Just then, a nurse came into the room with her medication and an aide arrived with her dinner.

"Why don't you go for dinner too," the nurse suggested. "We'll take care of her and make sure she eats."

I left the room in a daze unable to wrap my brain around what my mother had just told me. Was she telling me she blamed herself for her mother's death? My mind seemed to be overflowing with questions.

I thought about the story my mother told me about my grandmother's death. Hadn't she said the fetus was perfectly formed with ten perfect fingers and ten tiny toes? Was my mother telling me she felt responsible for the child's death also? Had she been blaming herself all these years?

Was she telling me something or asking for something? Had I missed an opportunity to help her? Had my lack of compassion caused her to retreat inside her own mind?

Sitting alone, I thought of that day in my childhood when I walked out of confession, feeling something I could not quite identify. Certainly, I felt relief and gratitude after confessing my sins, but there was more to it than that. Suddenly, I realized what I felt that day was joy.

Had my mother found any relief in telling me her secret? In "confessing" her sin, had she been able to forgive herself? I could only hope she had.

Then like a bolt of lightning, I had another, even more astonishing thought. I thought about how since childhood I had been blaming my mother for putting me into the hospital. Now I found myself thinking about my grandmother's death and about how adamant my grandfather had been in insisting his wife *not* be taken to the hospital.

Had my mother insisted on putting me into the hospital to give me a chance, a chance her own mother never had? Of course, I couldn't answer that question, and now, neither could my mother.

I wasn't there when my mother died. It was January 14, 2006, one month shy of her ninety-second birthday. As soon as Joanne called, I drove to the nursing home. When I arrived, I saw Joanne, her daughter, and my youngest sister Ronnie, standing at the foot of the bed, crying. I walked to my mother's side and put my hand on her arm. As a child in Catholic school, I had been told the spirit remains for awhile after death. I wanted that to be true. If it were, I wanted my mother to know I was there for her.

Afterward, I got back into my car and felt compelled to drive back down the highway, all the way down and into the city. When I got to the house we moved to in West Oak Lane, I got out of the car and walked up the steps, thinking about what Thomas Wolfe had said, that you can't go home again. As I rang the doorbell, I wondered if I had ever truly left.

To my left was the patio my father had built so many years ago where I'd spent so many hours sitting under the awning, reading or watching the summer raindrops falling all around me. Further out was the spot where the weeping willow tree had been, where I used to lie on summer evenings to look up at the stars.

"Who's there?" a voice called from behind the door. I explained myself as best I could. Of course, I was a stranger to its occupant who would not open the door, but spoke to me from behind it. It hardly mattered. I could close my eyes and remember every inch of space inside. The woman gave me permission to walk through the gardens.

In the side yard, I looked up at the window to the bedroom I had shared with my sisters. It was on the other side of that window where I had first struggled to understand death, where often at night, I would sit up and stare out, too afraid to lie down and close my eyes. Then one night, Gina told me an old wives tale, saying if you looked out a window and saw something white floating by, someone you knew would die. After that, I was more afraid of keeping my eyes open.

On the night my mother died, I dreamt I was walking home from St. Raymond's, taking the exact route I took as a child. At the end of the last street, I looked across at our front door. I crossed the street, climbed the steps, and after entering the house, saw my mother standing in the living room, looking not as she did when I was a child, but as she had just before she died.

"Mama," I asked, "how are you?"

"I'm all right," she answered. I woke up, feeling relieved.

"Dr. A," I said the next time I saw him, "when Joanne told me my mother had died, the first thought to pass through my mind was that we were in a dance together, my mother and I.

"Two weeks ago," I told the mourners at church during my mother's funeral, reading from the eulogy I had written for her, "my daughter Cindi invited me to go with her to an antique shop near her home in Langhorne. The building we went to was itself an antique, with odd-shaped, curtained windows and a lot of little cubby holes in out of the way places. It had at least three floors with narrow staircases and an endless number of rooms and it immediately propelled me back to my childhood home.

"Everywhere we went in that shop, I heard myself saying things like, 'We had one of those' or 'My mom had the exact same thing in our house when I was little.'

"It wasn't just my eyes that feasted on the past that day. My heart, too, returned to my childhood home, and I could remember times when I felt warm and protected there. And as I remembered those feelings, I allowed them to wash over me and bring me a feeling of peace I am still feeling.

"As an adult I had not remembered those feelings from childhood. As an adult, the space between my mother and me seemed to constantly narrow and often appeared seamless. But after that day, I was able to begin seeing myself as separate from my mother, and my mother as separate from me and from the relationship we shared.

"But if I never knew my mother as an individual, if I was never able to separate her from her role as mother, there is something I knew and have always known and recognized in her and that was her strength. My mother had enough strength to hold herself up under any circumstance and to hold up every person here in this church.

"My mother has moved on now. She has joined Aunt Nancy, Uncle Nicky, Uncle Domenic, Aunt Jenny, and all the others who left before her, especially *her* mother and *my* father. But she has left something of herself behind, something for all of us. She has left us her strength."

"When I woke up this morning," I told Dr. A the following week, "I awoke from a dream in which my ex-mother- and father-in-law were talking to me about my wedding ring. In real life, my wedding ring slipped unnoticed from my finger two weeks before Nathan and I separated, while I was washing clothes at a Laundromat.

"In the dream, my parents replaced my in-laws. My mom and dad looked like they did at about the time I lost the ring, but in the dream, I was aware that they had died.

"My parents had disowned me when I married Nathan, but in the dream, they told me they were going to find the ring and bring it back to me.

"'But you don't even remember what it looks like,' I said. They assured me they did. I watched as my father lifted an arm, grabbed something from the air, then opened his hand, and showed the ring to me.

"Dr. A, as I looked at my ring, I saw details in it I hadn't thought about in years."

"And how did you interpret that dream?"

"I took the ring to represent wholeness. I thought the dream meant my parents were wishing me well."

WHAT WAS IN
THE CHASM

In our next session, Dr. A and I again talked about the chasm I leave between the rest of the world and myself. When I told him I saw nothing when I looked across it, he again told me there was more to it than I was willing to see.

Even so, I felt ill-prepared for what happened later that day when I went to lunch at a fast-food restaurant not far from the bus garage. Although the romantic relationship between Vincent and I had ended, I continued to join him every day in his bus before our morning runs began.

That day, after therapy, I was standing in line, getting ready to order, when I looked out the window and saw Vincent's bus stopped at a red light. I ordered then turned back again. The light had changed, and as I looked at the empty space where Vincent's bus had been, I realized it was not his leaving that caused me to panic. His leaving caused me sadness. The panic was caused, not because Vincent wasn't there, but because I wasn't *here*. I suddenly knew there was no me for Vincent to come back to.

There was no me across the chasm because I had never been present in the first place. As a child in the hospital, I had constructed a false self, one I may as well have made with paper and scissors and had allowed that self to interact with others and only in the most superficial of ways.

"So where is your authentic self?" Dr. A asked when I told him what I'd learned.

I thought for a moment before I answered, "In the chasm."

"Then we'll have to go in and get you out," he said.

"We can't," I said, beginning to panic.

"Why not?"

"Because it's filled with—" I stopped, feeling foolish over what I was about to say.

"With what? What's in the chasm?"

"When I built it, I filled it with quicksand," I said, and we both laughed.

"It's okay. I'm an expert at removing people from quicksand."

"Dr. A, do you remember when I told you that the entire universe is made up of the same substance?"

"Yes. Was it quicksand?" he asked, still smiling.

"No. It was compassion," I told him as I smiled too.

I had my final session with Dr. A, in January 2008. Together we had taken therapy as far as we could go. I had learned a lot about my childhood and myself. As a child in the hospital, I had spent a whole year waiting. I waited for someone to rescue me and for someone to love me. I had spent the entire year feeling like a child not even a mother could love. Now I realized that I had believed that if Vincent had loved me, it would have proved my mother was wrong, and I would be, after all, irrevocably lovable.

I realized too, that if my mother's emotional growth had been stunted when she was sixteen, mine had been stunted when I was seven, but unlike my mother, I had the advantages of therapy and Dr. A.

Together, he and I had discussed all the spiritual masters. More than once, he had told me I needed words. I knew he meant that as a child, my mother had been so inconsistent with me that I never trusted myself to learn to read people. The unspoken signals people give to one another are a mystery to me. It's almost as though there is a language between people I can never hope to understand. Before meeting Dr. A, I barely knew it existed.

I knew, too, that he meant I needed words for reassurance and understanding, but my love for words went even deeper. As therapy ended, I could not resist asking some final questions.

"What should I do now?"

"I think you should write."

"What should I write about?"

"Write anything," he said. "Not just in your journal. I think you should write books. I can see a whole shelf full of books with your name on them. Write about God. Write about yourself. Write about anything. Just write."

I began writing almost immediately, and as I wrote, I realized I was still thinking about Vincent.

IN A DANCE TOGETHER

Two years after I stopped seeing Dr. A, Vincent and I got back together again. This time, we remained together almost constantly for an entire year. Then suddenly, unexpectedly, Vincent, who had always had his own demons and his own reasons for ending the relationship between us, ended it again, and I was left once again feeling like a princess who had been banished from her kingdom.

In the intervening two years, both Dr. A and I had moved, each of us putting more miles between us. This time when I returned to therapy, it was with a woman named Barbara. During one of our earliest sessions, Barbara told me I had an "adjustment disorder with anxiety." Although I had agreed with that diagnosis at the time, it seemed less than adequate. At a later appointment, Barbara told me about another of her clients who mentioned that a psychiatrist had diagnosed her with RAD. "As she talked," Barbara said, "I thought about you."

Barbara continued talking, telling me that RAD, or reactive attachment disorder, is a rare and rarely diagnosed disorder that begins in childhood. "It can last a lifetime," she said. RAD occurs when the emotional bond between a child and a parent is missing or when a child is abruptly separated from their primary caregiver, as I was when I was hospitalized at the age of seven.

Bingo, I thought. Finally, I had a name for what was wrong with me.

"Children with RAD," she said, "find it impossible to form normal attachments in relationships." As she went on to describe symptoms that included feelings of abandonment and inadequacy in all social situations, I remembered a conversation Vincent and I had back in 2002 when I was finding it difficult to express myself.

I wanted to tell him what I was feeling, but I couldn't. Instead, I wrote my feelings in a note and left it for him to find.

"What's wrong with you?" he demanded one sunny day in April, his words making the smile vanish from my face.

"What do you mean?" I stammered, feeling as though I had just been nailed. *How had he guessed my secret?* I wondered, not knowing it myself.

He smiled and his voice softened. "Why do you leave me notes then run away?" he asked as I felt relief and managed to smile again. But I had no answer.

Listening to Barbara that day, I finally understood why.

Then I remembered something else, something that had happened more recently. Although Vincent and I remained friends and stayed in contact, sometimes weeks or even months would pass before we spoke or saw one another again.

One day, I spoke with him late in the afternoon just as I was leaving work. He told me he had been out all day and after arriving home, had found a note taped to his front door and another identical note taped to his kitchen door.

The notes were from his doctor who said that the results of a blood test he had taken earlier that day had come back with a creatine level that was highly abnormal. He was instructed to go to the ER immediately. He told me his neighbor was taking him to the hospital.

"I'll meet you there," I told him. Knowing how long and agonizing the hours spent in an ER could be, I wanted simply to be there with him. I arrived as he was leaving triage.

The ER was unusually crowded that night and with no beds available, Vincent and I spent the night sitting on a gurney in a hallway. As doctors, nurses, orderlies, and patients walked past us and IV fluids trickled into his arm and through his veins, Vincent and I sat talking quietly together for hours. We talked until well after midnight when his blood test came back normal and he was free to leave.

On the ride back to his home, a companionable silence fell between us. I thought about how far I had come since the days when I had to write notes to express myself. As I pulled into his driveway, Vincent turned to me and said, "You were certainly stalwart back there." I smiled as I looked into his eyes and saw myself reflected there. I knew then that Rumi had been right when he said lovers don't meet—they are in one another all along.

As I drove toward my own home, I realized too that my closest, most intimate connection to another human being had just happened in a hospital. It was time to surrender and allow God to do his work and while I knew all of this, I could not help wondering why I had to go through all of it in the first place.

Then one day, while I was meditating, the answer suddenly came to me as I realized that God and I, too, are in a dance together.

I have turned seventy-two now, and as I continue searching for all the answers to all my questions, I know this much is true: I know the past no longer haunts me and the future no longer frightens me. And as for time itself, I know that there is no such thing as just once upon a time.

EPILOGUE

There are, I think, still too many questions, some of which I may
never have an answer for. But what I do know is that God is here,
right here, in the mysteries and synchronicities of my life.

—From my journal

HIS NAME WAS DON

It was raining lightly as I pulled into the parking lot of the first school on my afternoon run. Since I was early, I decided to sit back while I waited for my students to be dismissed. I closed my eyes, and while I listened to the rain, my thoughts turned to Vincent.

I couldn't remember the last time I'd seen him, although I had spoken to him just days earlier when he told me about his brother-in-law's death. "Fran had been sick for a long time," he said. His brother-in-law had lived nearby and Vincent had visited him often. "It was better this way," he said as I heard the pain in his voice and imagined him shaking his head in denial. I tried to comfort him, but felt the hopelessness that everyone feels when they are suddenly confronted with death.

Now, wanting to feel close to him again, I picked up my cell phone to call him. I dialed his number, but the call went straight to voicemail. I shivered. His phone had never done that before. Usually it rang, and he answered. This time he didn't. *What does that mean?* I wondered, trying not to panic. I had students to take home and knew that driving in the rain, which had gotten heavier, was going to demand all my attention. I closed my eyes and thought of calling again, but the sound of children running toward the bus stopped me.

It was after four when I finally arrived back at the bus garage. I had decided I was going to go straight to Vincent's house, but changed my mind. I would stop at the club first. The club was the Knights of Columbus where he had worked after retiring from the school district. If something was wrong, someone there would know and I could prepare myself before I saw him.

I saw his car, a red GMC Jimmy he had owned since before we met. I thought of it as emblematic of him and called it his little red wagon. It was tucked back in a corner, not in its usual spot close to the door. I went inside and stood for a moment while my eyes adjusted to the darkness. *There he is,* I thought when I saw him seated alone at the far end of the bar. I could tell he was tired. He looked a little hunched over. His eyes were glued to the screen across the room.

"What are you doing here?" he asked, surprised to see me. I told him about the phone call. How his phone had gone right to voicemail. I was worried. I was scared, is what I didn't tell him, but he must have heard the fear in my voice.

He smiled, told me he had turned it off on his way to his doctor's office and had forgotten to turn it on again. As he talked, I realized I was standing too close to him, but I couldn't move. I stayed where I was.

"I wanted to see you anyway," I said. And as I smiled, he smiled too.

We talked. About his brother-in-law's death and the funeral.

"I should have been there," I said.

"What for? You didn't know him."

"But I met him. Several times, and besides, I know *you.* I should have been there for you."

He told me then about the stroke his best friend recently had, about how his friend had almost died. "But he's going to be okay. He's in rehab and going home soon."

We talked for another half hour until he looked away and said, "I'd better be going home." My heart sank.

"No," I said. I reached out and placed my hand on his. *Please, let me be the first to leave,* is what I thought, but didn't say. He must have sensed how I felt because he stayed. We talked. Caught up and talked a little more until I realized I had better get moving if I wanted to be the first to leave.

"Listen," I said squeezing his hand. "If you ever want me." I stopped, felt flustered and started again. "I mean if you ever need me," I stammered. *What am I saying?* I wondered. I was standing close to him. Still too close to him. But I didn't move. I couldn't move. There was something I wanted to tell him. Something important, but I was having trouble finding the words.

I started talking again. The words came rushing out of me. Later I couldn't even remember what I'd said. I could remember only that Vincent had smiled as I spoke. Had I told him what I meant to say? I must have because he smiled again. I bent down, kissed him gently on the lips, felt his hand squeeze mine, and walked away.

"Vincent" whose real name was Don, died four months later, on February 2, 2014. I heard about his death on February 3 when his son called me. I had spent that entire morning working on the epilogue for this book, which had just gone into production with the publisher. On that morning, despite the fact that I had been using the name Vincent for several years to protect his privacy, I kept typing Don's real name instead. Later I wondered if he had been standing there beside me making me type Don instead of Vincent, and telling me, once and for all, that although he had to be the first to leave, I had not been abandoned.

February 8, 2014